My Lost Years

By Susan Kelly

and Sheila Jump

I'm a living corpse.

I was born with no feelings.

I am immortal, I can't die.

That was my mantra,
 my fixed belief.

I was sectioned and stayed locked up in a mental hospital
for nearly ten years………..

This is my story.
Maybe it will give someone hope, because,
I survived.

Introduction

Extract from my hospital notes, August 2002. *Susan remains on 5 minute observations. Has assaulted others on numerous occasions requiring Susan to be restrained using approved C&R techniques. Attempted to leave by snatching staff member's keys and swipe card – not for the first time. Remains a high fire risk.*

Woooomph, bang……one minute you are trying to leave the ward for a breath of fresh air, next you are face down on the floor being held down by five big nurses.

Imagine how that would feel, pinned down, barely able to breathe, not a clue what is going on, how long you will be there, feeling so bloody scared that you wet yourself. It's a fucking terrifying experience, even when you believe that you are immortal and can't die.

C&R is shorthand for control and restraint, which is a technique used by mental health staff to prevent someone from hurting themselves or others.

That someone was usually me.

In 2002 I had been on a locked psychiatric ward for two years. I was 43, I had allegedly set fire to bins, hit patients and staff, and I repeatedly said that I was a living corpse, born with no feelings. I would often ask staff to let me off the ward so that I could prove to them that I couldn't die. I wanted to walk out into a busy road or jump in front of a train. They didn't believe I was immortal so wouldn't let me out, so bloody frustrating.

I'm 65 now and want to tell my story because it might help someone else who is only just beginning their journey towards recovery. And this *is* a story of recovery, a story of hope.

I acquired my NHS notes, dozens of boxes, by requesting them under the Freedom of Information Act. It's been interesting, to say the least, to sift through them, if not bloody depressing too, because I only remember snippets of those years.

I can't believe some of the stuff written about me. I must have put my family, friends, and the staff, through hell, possibly one of the most difficult patients they ever had.

I'm so grateful for their patience and perseverance because I wouldn't be here today if it wasn't for them. I had more social workers/care co-ordinators than hot dinners. Sheila was the last of that long line. Professionally she stayed with me for seven years, is now retired, and is helping me to write this book as my friend.

Childhood memories

My name is Susan. I was born in 1959 at my grandparent's house on Chester Street in Blackburn, Lancashire. At some point later the family moved to Redearth Rd in Darwen, before settling at Rothesay Road, Blackburn. We had to move from there because my younger brother had bronchial asthma and the house was very cold and damp. So, we finally settled at Oban Drive.

I was the second child of Spencer and Margaret. My parents lived in London when my older brother was born but came back to Lancashire in 1959. My mum was from Lancashire originally and my dad, who was fifteen years older than her, was from London. They met when he came North looking for work. He was married before to a foreign woman, but I know nothing more than that.

There were four of us kids, me, my older brother Spencer, my younger brother Stephen and my baby sister Linda. I shared a bedroom with Stephen for most of my childhood and I always felt closest to him. There was roughly three years age gap between each of us.

In the house I remember most clearly, at Oban Drive, there was a kitchen and living room, mum and dad's bedroom, mine and my younger brother's room, little sister still in with my mum and dad, and my older brother had a room to himself. It was nothing posh but you don't know that when you are little, I don't remember even comparing it to my friend's houses until I was a bit older.

My younger brother Stephen was always rooting about in places he shouldn't and one day came down the stairs and announced, *"we're all friggin' bastards, they're not married"*, pointing at our mum and dad! The room was silent but neither parent said anything except to tell Stephen off for snooping!

I don't think they ever did get married. I know Mum was very jealous of Dad's first wife for some reason. I'm not sure that my Dad would be considered much of a catch, short and stocky and so much older than her, but she obviously must've seen something in him and was possibly worried he would go back to his legal wife. They argues like cat and dog, cheated on each other, but stuck together until death parted them.

My dad was bald for almost all the time I knew him but I do remember him getting measured for a wig, by a man who came to our house. I sat watching as the man cut a piece of dad's hair off to get a good colour match for the wig. I don't remember ever seeing him wearing a wig so who knows if he actually bought it or not!

I never met my dad's parents because they died before I was born. I did see a photo' of his mum, a tiny Irish woman called Elizabeth, sat in a deckchair on the beach at Blackpool. She died of tuberculosis, or TB. Her husband Arthur couldn't cope with his grief so bought a load of aspirin, got on a train to Brighton, booked himself into a hotel and took his own life.

No idea why he chose Brighton! He must have loved my granny very much to be unable to live without her. I saw a photo of him when I was older and he was a very handsome man. He was a tailor, a good job at the time, and I remember my dad getting upset if he ever talked about his mum and dad. In any future assessments of my mental health, the fact that my paternal grandfather took his own life, would be counted as a risk factor in the likelihood of me doing the same. Bloody hell.

My brother Stephen always got up to mischief, and he would often drag me into his plans. We hid under mum and dad's bed on one occasion, as he said he wanted to show me something. I was only about six. We waited until there was nobody else around and then we climbed up to the loft, where all of our Christmas presents were hidden!

He told me that there was no such thing as Father Christmas, that it was our parents who provided the presents and ate the things we left out for Father Christmas, and the carrot for his reindeer. I hated him for saying that!

Stephen was always up to something. He was grounded once and locked in our bedroom. Come to think of it, I must have been locked in there with him!! He said to me, they can ground me all they want but watch this Susan, and off he went out of the window, down onto the wash house roof and ran off! He was totally different to my older brother who always had his nose in a book, studying everything going on around him.

My dad was a horrible drunk. We all knew to keep well out of the way if he'd had a skinful. He was never violent to us kids, but he had a roaring shout that would waken the dead.

He had two bikes and a three-wheeler car outside the house and used to take my mum to work. One day he drove through a red light with my Nan in the car and nearly killed them both. She never got in the car with him again, calling him a bleedin' maniac!

One of my clearest memories is of being in hospital when I was five or six and being brought home in an ambulance. I'd had dysentery and was kept in isolation. Is dysentery still a thing these days, I don't know! I do know that I was frightened of everything after that. It must have been a fucking traumatic experience to leave me with such anxiety. I thought my mum and dad had sent me away because they didn't want me anymore, not because I was ill!

That was possibly the earliest beginnings of my mental health problems, and my friend Pauline said that I regularly talked about it even when I first met her at the age of eleven, so it was clearly a traumatic event in my young life. I must have had the personality type that made me more susceptible to anxiety, maybe.

Childhood visits to the dentist were also traumatic, sitting in the big chair with the weird smells of the surgery. We didn't really have many sweets because we couldn't afford them, so probably had ok teeth, but I clearly remember I had to have a tooth taken out at Larkhill Health Centre.

I recall the mask being put over my face, a weird smell, hissing of the gas, and falling asleep. I was told to count but then suddenly I was awake again. I remember the feeling of going to sleep under the gas, seeing lots of colours and weird noises, so yes, definitely another traumatic event.

Me and my Dad went home from the dentist on the bus, the old green Blackburn Corporation buses with the open entrance at the back and a conductor taking our fares. I remember lying on my bed when we got home, tasting the blood in my mouth.

I was scared of the bloody dentist forever after that because I thought they would put that mask over my face again, and even the thought of that made me panic. I remained terrified of the dentist from that day until well into my fifties. The fact that I still remember that so clearly shows how traumatic it was at the time.

I was scared of so many things as a child!

After that extraction, I was fed soup and porridge as I couldn't eat anything hard. My brother asked me what it was like having the tooth out and I remember telling him it was horrible! He said he was never going to eat sweets again but I said I was, but I would make sure I cleaned my teeth before bed! I assured him that he would be ok as he had better teeth than me, me now being a proper authority on dentistry!

I liked to chew bacon rind but once got it stuck in my throat and my Dad stood me on a chair and pulled it out! I never ate bacon again as the thought of choking on it frightened me so much. I was still quite young at that point but already the anxiety was becoming a fixed part of my life.

I remember being a bridesmaid for someone on my Dad's side of the family, no idea who, when or where! I had a long pink and white dress, which was so pretty. The bride wore a suit and a hat. I had a bouquet with a ribbon, and flowers in my hair. I remember feeling so special, and happy but not pretty, I never felt pretty.

After the wedding, I got a present for being a bridesmaid, a necklace. I had photographs taken but sadly no longer have them. I own very few photographs of my early years, or my family, but do wish I still had them. Sadly, I have no idea where they all went though some were lost in a house fire many years later.

Holidays were not a regular occurrence as we were not a well off family, but I do remember that once we all went to Pontin's near Blackpool for a week. Breakfast was served in massive dining halls, though probably a lot smaller than they seemed to me at the time. We played with boats in the water, which my brother loved.

I remember playing in the shallow end of the pool as I still couldn't swim. I had a blue swimming costume and can remember shivering. I also remember my mum putting a big towel around me. My mum played bingo to win money or prizes but again, I didn't understand at the time, what the games were that she was playing, I just know she enjoyed it! I remember going into Blackpool to the fairground, but I was always too scared to go on any rides.

Another time, we went to Cornwall with some new friends and their mum. It was so different to Blackburn. Everything was so much brighter! There was a massive playground with sand everywhere. I don't remember my Dad going with us so he may have been at work.

The only other trip I remember going on, was to London, to visit one of my mum's stepbrothers. I think my older brother stayed at home so just three of us went with Mum. Not really sure why we went and as usual we weren't told!

Life in London was so different to ours. I was confused by the different names for mealtimes. At home in Lancashire, we had our dinner in the middle of the day not at night like they did in London! I'd never heard of lunch!

My Dad always seemed to be in trouble with my mum! He got a whippet from somewhere that he planned on racing to make money, but he never did, I don't really remember why. I don't know what my Dad did for a job, but I do know that one day an ambulance turned up and took him away! It was the full on two men in white coats job and I remember it so clearly!

Apparently, it was something to do with his mental health and my mum got him locked up because she said "he wasn't right in the head" and not fit to be around us kids. I was seven at the time and remember him crying and banging his head on the wall.

My mum would say he would come home when he was better, and that it would be soon, not to worry, but of course worrying was all I did.

Days and then weeks went by. As a young child the days pass without knowing how long it's been. I have no idea how long he was away, but it must have been a long time, and my mum just carried on as if nothing had happened. I think we went to visit him but can't remember if that is a real memory or it is just what my mum told us. She said he was jumping from bed to bed in the ward, like a proper maniac. So mental illness definitely ran in the family on Dad's side, and a few years later, I would be next.

Dad

School

I moved to a Protestant school shortly after one of our house moves, mainly because my mum wasn't Catholic, but Dad was and he had insisted I went to a Catholic one to start with. I would think that the Catholic school wouldn't have let us in when they knew my parents were not married but living in sin! It was only a short walk to school. I seemed to fit in well but I was a quiet, observant child, not academically brilliant.

At primary school I loved the bottle of milk we were given every day. We would go into assembly every morning, where the headmistress would say prayers. I've never been religious and we didn't go to church as a family when I was little.

I liked school, especially as it was only down the road so wasn't far to walk. Junior school was a bit farther away but I walked by myself from the age of seven. I don't remember anyone ever taking me, but I must have been shown where it was! I remember the smell of disinfectant in the toilets and carbolic, lumpy green soap and how the smell clung to my uniform so much I could still smell it at home.

I used to go to swimming lessons at the same time as a boy from down the road. Neither of us could ever swim, we would cling onto the side for fear of drowning. Everybody else were there swimming and we were at the side shivering. Our birthdays were on the same day and he once got a toy Dalek!

Moving to junior school is another new chapter in life isn't it, but I didn't ever do very well at any school so was never that interested in learning. I was much more interested in playtime than whatever we were meant to be learning in the classroom, that was just boring stuff!

There was a nit nurse who regularly came to school to inspect our hair. I was sent home more than once because I was crawling with them. I used to pick them out of my hair and crack the nit eggs between my fingernails. Disgusting!

For some reason, I don't remember very much else about my time at junior school except for nits and sewing class. Whatever it was we made in sewing, mine was always rubbish compared to everyone else's. How on earth I got to a standard where I would get a job sewing handbags when I left school, I have absolutely no idea! One time when I was twelve, I hid something I'd made in the bin when I got home from school, but my mum found it and asked why I had thrown it away. I told her I couldn't do it and it was rubbish. I don't even know what it was. I certainly don't ever remember her saying that it didn't matter, or I was good at other things, like other mums would do.

I always enjoyed Music and Movement, which was like PE, but we had the radio on with music to move to! I knew my times tables because my Dad would go over and over those with us. I never went to a library because I just wasn't interested in reading. I did try to join the choir once, because it was raining outside of school and I wanted to be indoors, but I didn't pass the audition! I'm still in contact with lots of friends from my school days!

When I was eight I became close friends with a girl down the road who was a Catholic, and because of the nice dresses she always wore, I wanted to be a Catholic! Why on earth I thought that was why she had nice things, I'm not sure!! We were really good friends and played hopscotch and skipping and other stuff.

We would buy "scraps" every week and swap them with each other. Scraps were pictures of things, not from magazines but they were just pictures of a variety of nice things that appealed to us girls, bought in a pack from the local newsagent's shop. Can you imagine giving such a thing to kids these days!

I have lots of good childhood memories. I don't want anyone to think that it was all bad. I remember a record player in our house with music blasting out all the time, the Beatles, Mary Hopkins, country singers and Jerry and the Pacemakers. I loved watching Sooty and Sweep on the telly but there weren't that many children's programmes on in those days.

Unlike my brothers, I hated Dr Who, the music alone would terrify me and I'd run off to hide under my bed covers. I still go back to that when I hear the music now!

Every Thursday night was chippy night and we also got a quarter of dolly mixtures afterward. It must've been pay day.

We went fishing in the big pond in Queen's Park, catching tadpoles in our little mesh nets. We put them in old jam jars and took them home, expecting them to change into frogs, but of course they never did, they just died, because we probably didn't look after them properly. I think making us walk so far was part of mum's plan to tire us out before bed.

Queen's Park hospital was originally the workhouse for the poor of Blackburn. It stood on the ridge of a hill, so it was visible for miles around as a warning of where you could end up if you didn't have a job or pay your bills.

As with many such large buildings it later became a hospital. Queen's Park housed the mental health wards and little did I know when we played happily in that same park as children, that I would end up in that very hospital for a long, long time as an adult. Good job we don't know what lies ahead.

One of my friends went to Brownies, but my mum never took me to anything like that. My friend would have her Brownie uniform on and I was so bloody jealous. She always seemed to be doing something or going somewhere like Brownies or Holy Communion, while I never did anything like that. She was always a happy kid, always going somewhere with her mum, who seemed to do such a lot of nice things with her.

Dead people

My mum took me to see people in coffins, family, neighbours, even people she didn't know but whose names she saw in the local paper's death notices.

I've no idea why I was the child chosen to accompany her on these morbid visits, or why she had such a fascination with viewing dead people. I do know now that it had such a dramatic effect on me as a child, that it showed itself in my delusional beliefs when I was an adult, locked in a mental hospital.

My mum regularly used to visit an old lady further up our street and I would go with her in the hope of getting a biscuit. My Mum knew everybody and would never go past without shouting "oooowee" to whoever we saw across the street. We were always in and out of peoples' houses!

On the last time we went to the old lady's house, I didn't know that she had died as I hadn't been told. She was in her coffin and I could not understand what the fuck was going on. I was terrified! My mum didn't say anything before we went, I thought it was just the usual, me having to sit listening to them talking.

When we got there, my mum told me to look at the lady in the coffin. I knew it was her as she looked like her but she was so still and looked white, and she had a trickle of dried blood on her mouth. My mum sat and had a cup of tea with the other lady who lived there, but I couldn't wait to leave.

I was so scared because I didn't know what was going on! I sat rigid, waiting for my mum to finish, and I didn't even get a biscuit that time! Why would she not tell me that the old lady had died but her body would be there at the house, so I would be prepared?

When we finally went home, I remember sitting looking out of the window for ages afterwards, probably trying to process what I had seen. It was a lady, the old lady from up the road, but she was in a big box, quiet and still. My mum never said anything about it, no explanation, and I remember feeling really bad about it, scared.

The feeling passed but the memory of the event came back to me on a regular basis, haunting my thoughts.

I've no doubt in my mind that visiting dead people in their coffins with my mum, was one of the causes of how mental illness presented itself later in my life. My delusional beliefs were based on death. I believed that I was a living corpse, that I was immortal. As an adult now, I really believe that this was a direct reference to the trauma of having seen so many corpses laid out in their open coffins during my childhood.

My mum clearly didn't think that it would upset me at the time as she never discussed it with me. I'm quite sure I was the only child of the four of us who was taken to view fucking corpses on a regular basis. Lucky me…………..

When my mum's grandma died, we all had to go down to her house, not just me. Randomly, I remember the roads being cobbled. The house was dark and felt awful. My great grandma's body was on her bed, with her arms folded, a cross had been put in her cold white hands. I remember the feeling of the atmosphere being awful, dark and oppressive and again very frightening for me as a child. Those memories never go away. It makes me feel sick even now.

My mum lived with her grandma when she was a child. My gran only had the one child, my mum. When my gran remarried, after the death of her first husband, her new husband wouldn't look after my mum so she had to go, as a child, to live with her gran, my great grandma. That possibly had a negative effect on her emotional development, who knows.

When I was a bit older, probably about nine, my step-granddad asked me to go into his bedroom with him. I didn't know what he wanted but it just didn't feel right, so I refused. When I told my Dad, he went round to see my step Grandad and I never went there on my own again.

It must have been part of normal life to some extent, seeing the dead bodies of people we knew, because at that time it was the norm, whenever a family member died, they would be in their coffin in the front parlour before the funeral, so people could come to pay their respects.

After my great grandma died there was of course a funeral and everyone was dressed in black. I didn't understand what the hell was going on and it was never explained! Why was nothing ever explained!

It seems clear now that neither my mum nor my dad picked up on my high levels of anxiety! If they did, they possibly didn't know what to do about it. I suppose anxiety wasn't a recognised thing in those days! Everything was doom and gloom, an unhappy feeling like being in a black hole, a feeling I would become all too familiar with as an adult as I became more and more mentally unwell.

Coming out of Grandma's funeral, life just carried on regardless. I realise that I struggled to understand and process these events as a child because nobody explained them to me. Combined with what now seems to have been an anxious personality type, my decline into mental illness, sadly, seems inevitable.

I don't think it was normal to be taken to see so many corpses and have wondered if my mum had some sort of peculiar liking for it. Her obsession with death definitely got worse during my teens, and even more after my brother Stephen died just a few years later. She would avidly read the obituaries in the local paper and attend funerals of people she didn't know.

Siblings and pets

When we were children, my older brother Spencer, had a tent that he put up in the back garden each summer and he was allowed to stay out all night in it. I was so jealous of him and his friends. He would probably be described as a geeky kid these days, always had his nose in a book. He left home when he was about nineteen and I was sixteen, to live with his girlfriend's family. We didn't really have a relationship of any sort and I have no idea where he is now. I did go with our mum to visit him in hospital when he had a near fatal motorbike accident as a young adult, but didn't maintain contact.

My sister Linda always seemed to be dressed nicer than me when I think about it now. She was five years younger than me but died in 2022 before she even reached 60.

She was very spoiled when we were little. She once hit my brother with a cricket bat and gave him a large lump on his head. She didn't get told off for it because she was the baby. She got away with murder and was very naughty, despite always having pretty dresses! I just remember her spoiling whatever I was watching on telly or whatever game I was playing. No matter what she did she never got in trouble, but the cricket bat was put away somewhere and we were not allowed to play with it again.

I don't even remember there being a huge row when she told our parents that she was pregnant at the age of fifteen, after a one night stand. She carried on living at home, with her baby, until she was in her twenties. When she got married, her husband refused to have the child so he continued to live with my mum into adulthood. I no longer have contact with him or my other nephews, although I did see them briefly at my sister's funeral.

Stephen was my second brother as I've said, three years younger than me. We were pretty close, went to the same school and I looked out for him. One day he soiled his pants while at school and was crying. I took him home and got him changed and cleaned up and we returned to school. Stephen had bronchial asthma so always seemed to be ill. He was on medication from a young age and had to go into hospital even if he just had a cold.

All the boys on the street had marbles and played inside and outside the house. Stephen always played to win! Everyone had duds, alleys, and aggies. He would polish his marbles which were every colour under the sun, always shiny, and kept them in a cloth bag.

Considering we had very few toys, no mobile 'phones or screens, I don't ever remember feeling bored. Don't think I even knew what that meant!

When we were teenagers, Stephen was arrested and sent to prison. He regularly stole things, including cars and had obviously done it enough times by then to be sent to Preston Prison. I was so upset.

When we were young we always had pets. Not long before Stephen went to prison, we had an Alsatian dog called Rinty, a really massive dog. He joined in our games all the time. My Dad took him to the pub every weekend and would buy him a pint of Guinness. A local Policeman wanted to buy the dog to train him for work, but my Dad refused.

When Rinty became unwell we weren't allowed to touch him as he was aggressive, snapping and drooling all over the place. The vet said that he had throat cancer and he had to be put to sleep. He always used to lie across the top of the stairs when we were all in bed, protecting us.

When he had been put to sleep the house seemed so quiet. Weeks after he died my mum complained that there was a fresh pile of dog hairs at the top of the stairs. She said Rinty must have come back to reassure us he was ok but I was terrified of a ghost dog!

We also had a cat called Tiddles. He got run over by a bus. I had a diamond cross, no idea where I got it from, but when I saw someone had put Tiddles' body on top of the bin, I put my cross round his neck. Every day I would look out at the place where my mum eventually buried him, waiting for him to scrabble his way out. I'm surprised she didn't put him in a fucking coffin in the front room considering how much she seemed to enjoy death!

I was so distressed, losing both pets so close together and experiencing more death first hand. Death seemed to be everywhere. A girl in our class was knocked over and killed by a bus that dragged her down the street. I didn't even try to process that.

Secondary school

In 1970 I started at the local secondary school. I don't remember the 11+ exam that we all must have taken, but I obviously didn't pass or I would have gone to the grammar school. I had to have a new uniform, including a grey hat which I loved.

In class I met my friend Pauline for the first time. She was one week older than me, and we were the youngest in the class. We just looked at each other and I knew we would be friends, and we still are over fifty years later. I owe her my life.

Pauline remembers my house always being full of doom and gloom. My mum revelled in anything bad that happened to people. She would tell me things like *suchabody* down the road had gangrene and had to have her leg amputated.

Pauline reminded me of an occasion where the kettle at my house wasn't working and my Dad mended it with sticky tape.

Me and Pauline would go to the youth club at Shad centre because it was the only place we could go where there were lads, before we were old enough to go in the pub. My Dad came into the youth club one day, waving a bra about that he had got for me! I was mortified!!! Why did he do that!

Pauline recalls me always being on a diet, so to help me out at school she ate my puddings! I only ate savoury things because I believed they wouldn't make me fat. It must have been puberty that made me begin putting weight on because before that I was skinny, wishing I could be fat like my other friend. We made skirts at school but mine didn't fit as it took so long to make. Pauline's mum used hers as a dishcloth!!

For many years my mum continued visiting houses where someone had died, to offer her sympathies and to view the body in the coffin. For a long time, I was very angry towards her when I became unwell in my twenties, because the focus of my delusional beliefs was death. Early on though, I didn't know that was why I was so angry with her, because my brain just couldn't put it into words.

As a child I watched my mum putting her make up on, standing in front of a mirror in the kitchen, and I would pretend to do the same. I have always loved make-up and if I go for a day or so without putting it on now, I have to check myself, that I'm not becoming unwell, as that's often one of the first signs of relapse.

The first time my mum had an affair, she planned to leave my dad, when we were all still quite young. I was probably about ten, but not sure. She took us to another house where this fella was, and his wife!!! It was terrible! My anxiety was sky high and I just wanted to get out of there. We only stayed one night because Stephen became unwell and needed to go to hospital, so afterwards we just went back home!

She had a few affairs over the years, my mum. She would be out at the pub every Friday night, after having her hair done. My dad worked nights at that time.

I remember one occasion when she came downstairs dressed in a yellow halter-neck dress and asked me how she looked. I said she looked like a bumble bee, with her dark black hair and yellow dress.

I remember a different occasion when my mum was out and dad at work, and I saw her through the window, going into a house belonging to a woman across the road. The woman was with her ex-husband and my mum was with another fella. I can't have been more than eleven at the time, but I knew right from wrong!

I ran over the road and banged on the door saying I could see her and I knew what she was doing. I felt sick. Eventually, she came home but nothing was said, - was it ever! My dad came home the next morning from working nights. I don't think they really wanted to be together at that time, or my mum was bored and her men friends brightened her life up for a short while.

I have some very good memories of my dad. He had a motorbike and would wear a really thick coat when he went out on it and a crash helmet. He had painted a stripe on the helmet, with nail polish!

When I arrived home late from school one day, he was stood at the front gate waiting for me. My mum did a teatime shift at the local chippy so dad would make tea for us kids at home.

As I approached the gate he asked where I had been and I had to tell him I had been in detention. He had kept my tea of chips, beans and spam fritters warm in the oven. He presented it to me, saying here's your tea, and then pushed my face down into the plate! I was dripping in fucking bean juice!

My brother had tried to warn me that dad was so mad because I was late home, but I didn't realise. My dad screamed at me that I was in fuckin' detention here now as well! Not funny at the time, but very funny to think back on now. It was yet another event to add to the list of unusual things that happened and contributed to my lack of self-worth.

At weekends we would go on the fields at the back of one of the girl's houses, telling parents we were staying over at another friend's house. We had tents and bought bottles of cheap cider. It was my first experience of getting drunk, although if you actually weren't drunk, you pretended to be so as not be left out.

At secondary school we were separated into different groups, graded by academic ability. Pauline was far cleverer than me. She says that I was always a bit slow, they always had to wait for me, and look out for me, as if I was a bit bloody simple! A few of us went to the cinema to see the Exorcist, frightened me to death but Pauline thought it was funny. I was so terrified of anything supernatural.

There were five of us who all ganged together at school. We went to the fair when it came to town. I was frightened of going on any of the rides so would hold the plastic bags of water containing the gold fishes that the others had won. We all had orange furry jackets which we would brush so they would stand out, full of static! We all wore "monkey" boots and "parallels", which were trousers. What a sight we must've looked!

I think I was twelve when my periods started. I had not been given any information about what was happening to me, other than what I picked up from my friends.

I shouted my mum up to the bathroom when the blood arrived in my knickers for the first time. I was fucking terrified, I thought I was dying! She calmly gave me a sanitary belt, a thinnish bit of fabric that went round my waist and had two hooks hanging down from it, one front and one back. These hooked on to the biggest piece of cotton wool you have ever seen, a sanitary towel.

It was covered in something like thin cotton or paper and was placed between your legs to catch the blood flowing out of your private parts. It was like walking round with a bloody brick between your legs!

You had to change them regularly so I was shown where they were kept, in a secret place in the bathroom, and then the used ones were thrown on the fire to get rid of them. Coal fires were the norm of course at that time, brilliant for getting rid of anything obnoxious like that!

That also reminds me of using cut up newspaper instead of toilet paper. There would be one new roll of toilet paper a week, but Dad was always complaining about the cost of them and how quickly it was used up! Well, there were six of us in the house! Anyway, his solution was newspaper, not a unique idea I know, but not one of his best either! It would probably have been the local Telegraph he used, after my mum had finished reading the obituaries.

I don't remember doing any exams before I left secondary school and I certainly don't have any qualifications, probably because we left before exams were taken.

Jobs and a stalker

When I left school at the age of 15, me and Pauline both got a job sewing jeans at a local factory. I was bloody hopeless. My machine once set on fire and the boss said she had no idea why, because I didn't work that fast! There were endless rows of industrial sewing machines in that factory – the noise!

We were given our pay packets on a Friday, by one of the supervisors. A small brown paper packet with your name on it. It was always cash because no-one had a bank account. I didn't see a cheque book until well into my twenties! I was pretty good at budgeting and managing my money and still am.

When I was 18 and worked at the handbag factory, a very bad thing happened to me, a fucking stalker. One night I was stood in a bus stop in Darwen and a lad I didn't know was there. I had a green duffle coat on with a Boomtown Rats badge pinned on. I loved the Boomtown Rats. He pointed at my badge saying he liked the group. He asked me what my name was so I told him, Susan.

He asked if I wanted to walk to the next bus stop because the bus was a bit late. I said no, I'm not walking. He walked off and I thought I was shut of him, but that was just the beginning of it as the next morning, he was waiting when I got off the bus outside work. He asked where I'd been. I said I'm just going to work what do you mean where've I been. He told me I was late, he'd been waiting for me, so I just passed by him, saying I had to get into work.

He then began writing letters to me, giving them to my friend to give to me. I went in a shop to get some lunch and he followed me in. I tried to hide but he said he could see me hiding and he began to swear saying I was taking the piss out of him. I said that I didn't even know him and he said yes you do, you were getting on a bus late at night and you were eyeing me up. I denied ever getting on the Darwen bus late at night.

At finishing time, I went home but was so scared of seeing him. He was so scruffy, and I thought he would rape me or kill me, and I was terrified. Terror is one of the scariest emotions to experience. I really was so frightened of dying but was convinced that he could and would kill me. From then on, I got on the bus with a friend but one evening she said she wouldn't be on the bus as usual in the morning, so I asked another friend to wait for me.

When we got off the bus the scary bloke was waiting again. He had brochures for Pontins and Butlins, popular holiday camps of the day. He told me I was going on holiday with him and when I said I wasn't going anywhere with him, he said yes you are! My friend told me to run.

Thankfully he didn't chase after me. It went on for a couple of months though, with him following me and it began to make me feel ill. I lost my appetite and I was so frightened of seeing him. He even told me he loved me and that he knew I loved him, but I didn't - he scared the fucking life out of me.

It carried on for about three months or maybe longer. I was too scared to go to the bus stop unless my friend was there. My brother came all the way from Burnley to pick me up a few times when I was really scared.

The Police became involved when I was off work one day. The man went into my workplace shouting where the fucking hell is she. The boss rang the Police and they visited me at home. I had to give them descriptions of him. Remember, this was in the days when stalking wasn't a recognised offence. It never crossed my mind to report him to the Police! Thankfully, I never saw him again after that but the experience left an indelible mark on my psychological wellbeing.

That experience took a lot out of me. My nerves were shot. Being frightened of someone you don't know, terrified he was planning to hurt me or even kill me. I have never ever seen him again, so I hope that means the Police got him or something else frightened him off. It took a long time for me to stop checking bus stops and I haven't used buses ever since.

Death

At the age of 19, I arrived home from work one day, to be told "Stephen died today." My 17 year old little brother had died in prison because he didn't have access to his inhalers.

He had suffocated to death having fallen out of bed in the hospital wing. He was all alone and was blue when he was found on the floor, with lots of bruises and scratches on the back of his hands.

I've no idea why he was alone if he was in a ward, or what the marks were, but the Inquest, obviously, said that there was no evidence of foul play or neglect on the part of the prison staff.

My mum had been to visit Stephen the Sunday before he died. I'd been out in the park that afternoon and experienced a weird sensation of being unable to breathe. I had an overwhelming feeling that Stephen was unwell, which mum confirmed when she got back. I usually went out on a Sunday night but didn't go that day. I still wish I had gone with my mum to visit him.

My immediate reaction when told that Stephen was dead, was to start banging things, anything I could get my fucking hands on in the kitchen. The pain of loss was overwhelming, like an actual physical pain, and I was so angry that this had been allowed to happen.

There was a postmortem and that delayed his body being brought to the local undertaker's. My mum was allowed to have him at home for the one night before the day of the funeral, with the usual set up of a coffin on trestles in the front room.

I couldn't bear it, the overwhelming grief, and I had become numb. I felt like I was in a bubble, in a different world from everyone else. How could it even have happened to him, and to me as well.

The house had to be kept cold while the body was there but there was still an overpowering smell of something nasty that stuck in my nostrils. My gran asked if I wanted to look at him, so I said yes.

It wasn't scary like I'd thought it would be, but so, so sad because he was so young. My mum and uncle stayed up all night with his body. My mum tried to lift Stephen out of the coffin to hold him, but he was too heavy.

At that time, we had a dog called Lassie who barked all the fucking time. When Stephen's body was brought in, he went quiet, and sat under the coffin until it was taken away again. Loads of people came to pay their respects, including family, friends and neighbours. I hated every one of them, coming to gawp, and was probably horrible and rude to all of them.

Stephen was buried in a local church yard and I remember the sound of the church bells slowly ringing. Loads of people came including two serving prisoners, Stephen's mates, both in handcuffs with officers chained to them. Our old head teacher was there as well. He was very kind in the way he spoke to me. I realise no that I had been feeling so alone in my grief because everyone else was wrapped up in theirs. We all dealt with it as individuals rather than a family sharing a terrible grief.

Stephen

As we were all standing around the newly dug grave at Stpehen's funeral, my aunty nudged me and said how bloody gorgeous the vicar was! I used to watch horror films with her sometimes, and she thought the vicar looked like her favourite actor, Christopher Lee.

I couldn't believe what I was hearing. I looked at her and just said, what the fuck…. She looked back and said well you've got to admit he's bloody fit! Unbelievable.

I'm convinced that Stephen's death sent my mum over the edge. Clairvoyants would regularly visit the house afterwards and if a lightbulb flickered at any time, she thought it was Stephen trying to get in touch. She was definitely more than a bit fucking weird after that.

After Stephen died, she was still buying him clothes and I told her he's dead, you don't have to buy him clothes! How do you get over losing a grown son though. It was hardest on her I know, but the rest of us suffered as well, not that mum noticed at all.

Romance

When we turned twenty one, Pauline and I had a joint birthday party. It was the typical rowdy sort of affair in a local pub, lots of beer, dancing, fags and snogging.

I'd already lost my virginity when I was fourteen when we were babysitting for Pauline's mum. I remember who he was, even his name, but won't mention it obviously. He had come prepared with a condom, hoping his luck would be in with at least one of us, cheeky git. I thought when he asked me to go in the bedroom with him, we would be having a cuddle!

I was so naïve, didn't have a clue what was going on, but I know it was fucking horrible. I will never forget the shock and pain of his dick going inside me. I cried and bled for days afterwards and kept having a bath, trying to get rid of the feeling of being dirty. I felt too guilty to say anything to my mum although I don't remember ever being told that sex was dirty, or something I shouldn't do, but I knew it was something I didn't really want.

I honestly don't think that anyone can appreciate what it means emotionally to do that as a young teenager, but sex was what all the girls talked about, keen to do it as quickly as possible, get it out of the way so we could brag about it to everyone else. I never really understood what it meant though until it happened, and certainly didn't understand making love until I was much older.

At the end of the party for our 21st, we moved on to the Cavendish club. I spotted a bloke, across a crowded room as they say. He was fucking outrageously, drop dead gorgeous and I couldn't keep my eyes off him, or my hands as it turned out.

He seemed to spot me at the same time and we moved towards each other through the crowd, and he bought me a drink. We danced together all night and I invited him back to my house.

I still lived at home with my parents, but it was ok to bring someone back as long as he didn't go anywhere near my bed. When I said I was going to change into something more comfortable, his eyes were out on fucking stalks. When I returned in my pyjamas and woolly dressing gown, he looked well disappointed. I brought him some blankets and a pillow and told him to make himself comfy on the settee.

I had no intention of sleeping with him when I had only just met him, no way. He was introduced to mum and dad the next morning when my dad tripped over his shoes and found him asleep on the settee.

I wasn't sure if I would see him again but when I got back from work later that day, he had left a big bunch of flowers, box of chocolates, a birthday card and a note saying he would see me later. Nobody had ever given me flowers.

When he turned up on the doorstep later, he asked if I would go out for a meal with him. That wasn't something that people like us did, go out for meals, so it all felt very grown up and a bit posh.

As I climbed up into his works van, I couldn't help but see all the tools in the back. In 1980 we were all becoming aware of the Yorkshire Ripper and were on our guard, even though we were in Lancashire! The feeling of excitement at being out with a more mature man far outweighed the potential worries on being murdered!

We carried on seeing each other for several months. Sex with him was so different to the experience I had with the spotty youth at Pauline's house. He was so gentle and kind and took his time when he realised I was inexperienced and scared.

After a few months, I had missed a period and then I started to feel sick all the time. I was in shock, oh shit, I must be pregnant. There were no instant tests in those days and I had to go to the doctor to have a test which took days and days to come back. The result was positive, I was pregnant.

I wasn't sure how he would react but told my lover that evening that I was pregnant. The colour drained from his face and I knew in that instant that my suspicions from the start were right.

He told me he was married, that's where he went every weekend, home to his wife and kids. This was not what he had planned – well me neither but here it is you pillock!

I told him to get the fuck out of my house, and out of my life. He said he hadn't told me he was married because he knew I wouldn't have gone out with him, but he really loved me. Too fucking right I wouldn't have gone out with him!

I threw him out. I felt so bad for his poor wife being treated that way. Had he lived in Blackburn it would have been so much easier to end it there and then. He actually lived down South somewhere and was working a contract in a town close to Blackburn. He carried on trying to contact me and I eventually gave in and we got back together a few weeks later, possibly because I was pregnant and I didn't know what else to do. My parents had no idea he was married and we managed to keep it that way for a long time. They would have been far more upset at that than me being pregnant.

At the same time that I was pregnant, my fifteen year old sister got pregnant on a one night stand. A few months into my pregnancy I had been out with my mates as usual, to the pub on a Friday night. I felt rough all day Saturday, worse than the usual hangover.

I stayed in bed until Monday morning but by then the pains in the bottom of stomach were so bad that I went down to Pauline's. Who knows why I didn't call an ambulance. By the time I got there we could see my stomach contracting and then I started to bleed. Pauline rang for an ambulance and I was blue lighted up to the hospital. I was 28 weeks pregnant; it was too soon.

By the time I was examined in the delivery room and had had my pubes shaved, common practice at the time, I began to feel that I needed to push. I was in the hospital a total of twenty minutes before my baby was born. He was so tiny; he was rushed away in an incubator.

I didn't get to touch him and I later refused to hold him when I was taken down in a wheelchair to the special baby care ward. His tiny body was covered in wires and he had a tiny hat on his head. I asked the nurse if he was going to die but all she said was that they didn't know yet. I didn't want to touch him because I knew he wouldn't be staying. Self-preservation maybe.

My baby lived for seventeen days. I named him Jonathan and I still think about him every single day.

Once again, only a year or so after my brother dying, I was eaten up by grief. I felt completely numb, couldn't think of anything at all. I didn't eat, I didn't sleep. I had to tell the baby's dad that he had been born too early and he came straight away. I don't even know if he held him or not. When I was discharged home, I wouldn't go back to visit and I wasn't surprised when I was told that my baby was dead. I felt nothing but all-consuming, overwhelming grief.

I could not face going to the funeral, still feeling so numb. His little body was put into a tiny white coffin. I've always assumed his dad paid for the funeral but don't know for sure. He told me later that the undertaker had put the little white coffin across his knees in the car and he had to then carry it to the altar in church. My mum went to the funeral and my dad stayed at home with me, at a loss as to what to do or say. I was 21.

Even though I knew about his wife and family, our relationship carried on after our baby died. We loved each other. He would stay with me at my parent's house and we were allowed to share a bed after the baby died, big deal. He was always good to my mum and dad, putting money in the electric meter and stuff.

He told me he was getting a divorce as it wasn't fair to stay his wife when he didn't love her anymore. He wanted me to go to meet his family. He had moved into a caravan and was building a house for himself. I would go to stay because I was no longer working but was on the dole.

When I met his mum and dad and wider family, I felt really uncomfortable, out of place, even though they were very nice to me. It was some sort of a family party where I met them, so there were friends there of his wife, and they were understandably unpleasant. Obviously neither she nor the children were there. I felt really bad that his children were missing out on a family party and that was the start of realising that the relationship had to end.

It still took a long time, but it did eventually end. I was down at the caravan one weekend, possibly early 1982, and he had loads of Valentine's cards around the place, and I mean loads! I asked him how many women he had on the go but he denied that, saying they were all from admirers. Admirers who knew where he lived. He distracted me with sex, sex that was always bloody fantastic, despite his horrible teeth which were brown and crooked. We sat for ages afterwards, naked, eating cheese and crackers with a bottle of wine. Very posh.

At about nine he said he had to go out to look at a job. Alarm bells were ringing so loud in my head – so many Valentines is not normal, looking at a job at nighttime, not normal either? He said he wouldn't be long and went out, leaving me with his massive fucking dog that lived with him. I got myself into bed and only realised when I woke up the next morning that he had been out all night.

I knew I'd been well played and that he must have been with another woman. By that time, he had moved on to another job away from Blackburn, so could easily have had another woman, if not more. I would only ever see him if I travelled down to his caravan.

When he finally got back, I could smell the other woman on him. He had no excuse for staying out all night. I said I was leaving. I accepted a lift from him because I had no money and no other way of getting home, but it was a long and silent journey.

We didn't actually say we were finished, that it was over, until much later. He rang me and asked if I had met anyone else. I was still reeling from losing the baby and then him, trying to accept what a cheating fucking liar he was to have even looked at anyone else, tosser. I told him that I would always love him but things were just not meant to be. I wasn't able to see his face but felt his relief down the 'phone line. I was twenty two but felt that I had already lived enough to cope with for a lifetime.

Problems

Shortly after the end of my relationship with Jonathan's dad, I began to experience a weird sensation of swallowing my tongue, choking on it. I hadn't been able to cry at all since my baby died.

I always thought I was the black sheep of my family and my baby dying added to that insecurity. My mum never ever told me that she loved me, not once. I felt so insecure and unloved. Me and Stephen were in the middle of the four of us. My older brother had the brains and my younger sister was definitely spoilt just because she was the baby. She went everywhere with my mum. I never went anywhere with her unless it was to view a fucking corpse.

Even when we were grown up my mum still preferred my brother and sister to me. It was like when my sister had her baby shortly after mine died, my mum was over the moon! She wanted to call the baby Stephen which I objected to. My mum got her way and from then on, my nephew was my brother's namesake.

My mum worked at the hospital on nights at that time. My sister would not get up during the night to feed her baby when he cried, so I had to do it. My mum, knowing full well that I had only lost my baby in May, three months before my nephew was born, left me to feed him. Nobody asked if I was ok with that, nobody seemed to suggest my sister should do it herself. It was so bad. I hated Linda at that point, and my mum.

My nephew was the result of a one night stand so I imagine that's why my sister never really bonded with him, but my mum did. She spoilt him. I gave my sister all of the baby stuff that I had bought for my baby. A pram, cot, bottles, sterilisers, nappies, everything. My mum just took over. I'm sure she thought it was my brother reincarnated.

Mum brought him up with my help because my sister was always out, often staying out all night. It was sad for me because my mum didn't think anything of the grief that I was going through and how bad it was to be looking after my nephew when I had only just lost Jonathan. Or maybe she thought it would do me good to be looking after my nephew, take my mind off my dead baby. She never said, like she never said much about anything.

One small bright point during that time was a friendship I had with a really nice bloke. I met him in the pub when I was pregnant with Jonathan, but I saw him as nothing more than a friend. My feelings were never strong enough for him, not enough to give up Jonathan's dad anyway but he was a nice kind man and I have wondered how things might have turned out if I had fallen in love with him. He's been happily married for many years.

When I finally went back to work, after Jonathan died, I had moved from the handbag factory to work in a slipper factory. I would sit in the toilets trying to get over the feeling that I was choking. I would sit with my tongue hanging out, then I would smoke until I felt the discomfort was passing and was able to go back to the factory floor.

I soon moved jobs again and went to work in a bridal factory. The manager was so nice there, so kind. I used to go out and wander around a nearby field on my breaks and he saw me through the office window. He called me into the office and told me he thought I wasn't very well. He said that I needed to go home and make an appointment to see a doctor. He finished me, but in a way that I was able to claim benefits straight away.

My GP prescribed Ativan, a benzodiazepine drug also known as Lorazepam. It is now known to be extremely addictive and doctors are now more careful in prescribing it. It is usually prescribed for anxiety and poor sleep.

In 1984, aged 24, I was first referred to a psychiatrist for my nerves. When I saw the psychiatrist, I told him that my problems began in February that year when I swallowed a piece of broken tooth. I felt as if there was something stuck in my throat. I was sent for an x-ray and even had an investigation under anaesthetic, but nothing could be found. The doctor said that I was possibly on the verge of a nervous breakdown because my throat was so constricted. Anxiety can do such weird things to our body.

Apparently, I also developed agoraphobia at that time, an extreme or irrational fear of entering open or crowded places, of leaving one's own home, or of being in places from which escape is difficult. I was scared of meeting people and at times felt that I was saying the wrong things to people. My life had changed completely since my baby's death, less than three years earlier. The dose of Ativan was increased.

A letter dated November 1984, from one of the doctors, said that in the past I was a very friendly and outspoken girl who used to mix well. Was I? I wondered who had told him that.

The psychiatrist talked to me at great length and he thought that I was suffering from an anxiety state that was causing the difficulty in swallowing that I still had and was my main symptom.

I was told to continue taking the Ativan at the same dose and was to be referred to the Clinical Psychologist. The psychiatrist said in the letter that they would be seeing me again.

And so it began, my journey into psychiatric care. I was 25.

Mark and Jake

I was assessed by a psychologist in January 1985 but according to her letter I reported that my difficulties in meeting people, and swallowing, had reduced considerably and I was a lot happier.

I had a new relationship with Mark, my future husband, and the psychologist said that he was probably helping me far more than she ever could, so I was discharged from the service.

When I was reviewed by the psychiatrist in February 1985, he too thought I was much improved. I wasn't working because I was expecting a baby in July.

I continued to live with my parents at Oban Drive. The psychiatrist recommended that I reduce the Ativan by half a tablet a week. He planned to see me in May just to keep an eye over me. When he did, I told him that I had continued to improve, no more swallowing difficulties or feeling that I had a lump in my throat. I had come off Ativan by myself, with no adverse effects.

The psychiatrist was very impressed that I had managed to come off the drug without any medical support and that I wasn't taking any at all, as that is unusual with it being so addictive. People often have to stay on a tiny dose forever due to it being so addictive. He had once told me that everyone has two sides to them and he was now seeing the well side of me. It was 1985 I was nearly 26 and I was pregnant for a second time. I was discharged from psychiatric services.

I had met Mark in a club in Darwen in 1983. No dating apps in those days! I had only just started going out again socially after finishing with Jonathan's dad, and I was in the Dancers pub with my group of mates. We were sat at a table when a dark haired, very handsome, not too tall man approached us and spoke directly to me. He had a big scar on his neck which I later found out was due to being scalded when he was little.

Cheeky sod asked if I would marry him the next day and invited me back to his, both of which I refused!! The next day one of my mates said that Mark had been asking around the pub about me, saying he wanted to take me out.

Week after week, no matter which club we went to, Mark was there. I found it difficult to talk, partly because of the high dose of Ativan I was still taking then. I felt that I was constantly swallowing my tongue and couldn't breathe properly. There was at least one time when I got a taxi home and couldn't speak to tell the driver where I lived and had to write it down.

Eventually, after a night in the Roxy, I went home with Mark. I was not on the pill so nothing happened that first night, but we did start dating after that. Even though it had been a couple of years I was still on the rebound from Jonathan's dad. I had felt nothing when we split up because I was still numb from losing the baby. The tablets do that to you as well, make you numb so that you are not feeling anything, good or bad.

I accused my mother of hiding the tablets once when I ran out of them. I spent all my time watching the clock, waiting for the time when I could take another tablet. I could feel it when the effect was wearing off and I felt that I was choking on my tongue again. The tablet gave me some relief for a couple of hours so when I realised the packet was empty, I went bonkers. I asked where they were, screaming at my mum to "give them back you fucking bitch."

I was on the floor in the kitchen crawling around on all fours, screaming and crying. She literally picked me up by the scruff of my neck and marched me to the GP surgery. She shouted at the doctor, asking him if he would prescribe this muck for his own daughter! I begged him for more and he gave me another prescription….. I just couldn't focus on anything. I was a benzo addict.

Anyway, back to Mark. He had a really good job at British Aerospace as a chaser. We dated regularly. We went to London to meet his uncle. Mark's parents didn't have anything to do with the uncle because he was gay. It was a funny, strange weekend! We took him a set of four brandy glasses as brandy was his favourite tipple. He seemed very pleased with them and welcomed me in like a member of the family.

It was after about eight months together, that I realised that I was pregnant. I was still seeing the psychiatrist but I began to wean myself of the Ativan as well as booze and cigs. I thought all of that might have contributed to losing my baby before, so I was going to be sure to cut everything out this time. At least Mark wasn't married to anyone else and he was quite chuffed when I told him I was pregnant. He wanted me to move in with him straight away but I wasn't so sure at first and stayed at my mum and dad's.

My sister was married by then and also pregnant again, so it seemed that there was very little reaction from my mum and dad when I told them I was expecting as well. I stayed at my mum and dad's right through the pregnancy. I don't remember either of them being over attentive, that just wasn't their style!

My baby was due on 12 July 1985. Having lost one baby, every week leading up to the twenty eight week point was torture. Once I passed that milestone, I should have been able to relax a bit but I couldn't. I was terrified and convinced that something would go wrong again. Nothing else occupied my thoughts and as my due date approached, I was absolutely off my fucking head with worry.

On 7 July I had been in for a check-up and they wanted to keep me in and induce labour. I begged them not to do that. I was terrified enough already without that. I was allowed home but a few days later, woke up feeling weird. I was bleeding and I fuckin' panicked. Pauline came round just as my mum rang for an ambulance.

My mum rang Mark at his work, while Pauline went with me in the ambulance. Pauline desperately wanted to stay with me through delivery and we agreed she could if Mark didn't arrive in time, but he did, just in time to see his son come out into the world. Childbirth is excruciatingly painful and I don't believe anyone who says different.

My mum arrived shortly after the baby was born. It was quite a quick labour but I was so scared that there would something wrong with him. I could not believe that he seemed perfect, all 8lbs 5oz of him. I had 4 stitches and was high on Pethidine, so told my mum to piss off home if she was going to sit there crying. We were no closer than we ever had been so I just didn't need her there! I named my baby Jake, and he is still the absolute world to me.

It didn't take long for my fears to become reality when I noticed a lump on the side of the baby's head. The nurses said it was due to the pressure of the birth canal on his head, but I was scared shitless.

I honestly don't think I can say I enjoyed having a new baby because I was so absolutely terrified that something bad was going to happen to him. Every visitor asked what the lump was, and I just cried even more. It did go away eventually but it all added to my anxiety.

I was moved to the local maternity home at Bull Hill and tried to breast feed, determined that this baby would have the best of everything.

Mark wanted me to go home with him rather than back to my parent's house. I just didn't know what to do, my whole focus was on this tiny new person that I was responsible for.

I didn't think I really wanted to leave home to go to Mark's but I did go eventually because I felt like I should because of the baby. All of my stuff was taken to his, and that is where me and the baby went, when we were discharged from the maternity unit.

Things were fine for a while but Mark seemed to change after the baby was born, almost as if he was jealous of the attention I had to give to Jake. I suppose, due to the high levels of my anxiety, it must have looked as if Mark was getting no attention at all.

I was convinced the baby wasn't getting enough milk from me. I sat and constantly watched him when he was asleep or awake, barely taking my eyes off him in case he stopped breathing.

Mark went back to work after a week or so. I realise now that I had post-natal depression. I didn't wash or get dressed, just sat staring at my baby boy. Having lived on his own for most of his adult life, Mark was pretty set in his ways. He didn't want me to cook his tea, although I did try to make a shepherd's pie one day but he didn't want that, he wanted chips so took over when he got home. Fine by me.

When the baby was only a few weeks old, he stopped feeding, convincing me even more that I was not doing it right. What a useless mother I was after all, couldn't feed him and couldn't stop him crying either! Fucking failure, just as I expected. He seemed to just cry and cry all the time.

Pauline helped out as best she could be she had two little ones of her own by then. I took my baby to the doctor who said he had tonsillitis. The scariest thing of all was that his neck began to swell up, and the bigger it got the more he cried.

When the Health Visitor came she took one look at both of us and put us in her car, which she made a point of telling me wasn't really allowed and took us straight up to the hospital. I was right, it was my fault. He had an ear and throat infection which he had got from my untreated mastitis. Untreated because I didn't even know I fucking had it, I just thought breast feeding was meant to be that painful!

The baby was taken straight to the operating theatre. I was convinced he would die and I would lose him as well because I clearly did not deserve a baby.

The Consultant who looked after him was so kind. He said that once they had anaesthetised the baby they were able to examine him properly and had removed loads and loads of pus from his throat and ear, so much so it had just poured out of his little ear. To add to my panic the doctor told me that the baby had stopped breathing on the operating table, but they were able to resuscitate him. I could barely breathe for fear.

My baby had to stay in hospital for about four weeks to be treated with antibiotics. I barely left his cot side. He still screamed at times but his little body was full of drips and needles and I think he was hungry. When he was finally allowed to start having a little bit of milk in a bottle he thrived!

During those few weeks nobody came to visit, not Mark, my mum, nobody. The doctor eventually made me go home for some sleep, a bath and a change of clothes. As I was leaving the hospital Pauline came in with her son who had fallen off a garage roof whilst playing. We both just looked at each other and I was able to feel some relief for a brief moment!

I didn't like going back to Mark's and once I'd slept for a bit I went straight back to the children's ward. I never asked Mark why he didn't come to visit. One of life's many little mysteries….

Once my baby was well enough to go home, we went back to Mark's again but I was very unhappy there. I was alone all day while he went to work, except for the times that Pauline would call in. How I would ever have survived without her, I do not know. She is the main reason I am still here on this planet at the age of sixty five.

I refused to let Mark look after his son. I became suspicious of where he was whenever he went to the pub. He used to get dressed to the nines when he went out. I started to sniff his clothes for perfume, really paranoid behaviour. As it turned out I wasn't far wrong. He was having a string of one night stands, just as he used to do before we were together.

A girl came round once, wearing a very skimpy top, trying to be my friend, but it was him she was after. He would walk her home. I found a birthday card from her in his jacket pocket. She even had the nerve to come round one day to tell me that Mark had tried it on with her in the club.

I never said anything about what she had told me, not wanting to cause trouble, but the next time we saw her while out, he blanked her. She assumed I had told him what she told me, so later told him everything herself, in case I had missed anything out! He came home so drunk and smashed every stick of furniture in the house.

Once he was asleep in bed I packed up and took the baby to my mum's house, again. I saw the girl again a bit later and she told me that she would be sleeping on my side of the bed now, bloody cow. I told her she was welcome to the lying, cheating bastard. He dumped her before she got anywhere near moving in with him, though I suspect she had been on my side of the bed a few times before that.

Pauline and Susan

Mark rang my mum's house almost daily, crying and begging me to take him back but by then I was planning on getting my own place. I knew that he was a drug addict and probably an alcoholic as well. I caught him injecting something once, sat on our bed with a tourniquet wrapped around the top of his arm.

I looked at him in horror and asked what the fuck he was doing. He said it was nothing to worry about and he would be downstairs in a few minutes. Was I really so stupid not to leave him there and then, flounce out, slam the front door and go back to my mums permanently?

Like so many women, possibly more so at that time, I was too scared to do anything. That's how people are controlled by others, by being made to feel scared, that they can't do anything or be anyone, unless they stay with that abusive partner, because that's what he was, I know that now, but all I knew then was I was terrified of upsetting him any more than I did by just existing.

When a friend of Mark's had come to stay with us from London, they had gone out to the pub while I stayed at home with the baby, coming back in the early hours. Mark came barging into the bedroom, looking for his drugs. He shouted at me that he would fucking kill me if I didn't give them back to him but I hadn't a clue where he had put them!

The baby was asleep in his cot in our bedroom and I was more concerned about him being woken up than some lost drugs. Mark went back down to his mates and began smashing beer bottles. I crept out of bed. I was so terrified he would hit me with a bottle, I was shaking from head to toe.

I remember I was wearing a night shirt and as I stood at the top of the stairs, pee ran down my leg onto the brown carpet. Mark's mate went round to one of the neighbours to get help and they were able to get me and the baby out to their house.

I went back to my mum's again and stayed there. In spite of everything it still felt like home. Mark rang over and over again, begging me to go back to him. When I eventually did, everything was forgotten and life was fine again for a while, as if Mark was trying to make it up to me and to behave like a proper husband and dad.

I never challenged him though about his previous behaviour because that just wasn't the done thing. Even in the 1980's domestic abuse was just between the couple. The Police would certainly not intervene if it was "just a domestic".

The peace didn't last long of course, he was an alcoholic and drug addict and couldn't function without either. I don't think I knew what an alcoholic was really, or that it was an illness. I just knew that my life was a misery. I wasn't working so relied on him for money. He gave me £5 a week which wasn't a lot even then, but he resented every penny of it. He liked to spend his money on himself.

Mark was a big drug user, had tried everything. I think I just pretended it wasn't happening, too terrified of the probable fallout if I did say anything to him. I thought he was just a heavy drinker, not that unusual, most men went to the pub regularly and got drunk, but he was an alcoholic, drinking whenever he could, he didn't just want it, he needed it and had bottles hidden all over the house.

After I had gone back to my mum's one of my neighbours rang me and said that Mark was in a bad way. I said so was I! I was scared of what he might do to us but eventually agreed to go back to him. I must've been off my rocker, or I really did love him, I really can't say which. I was living on my nerves, constantly on high alert for what was going to happen to me next.

For a while everything was hunky dory once again. Mark wasn't using drugs every day and my anxiety eased a bit. I even started to believe that my baby might not die after all. Of course, none of it lasted for long, I'm sure you've got the picture of me by now…..

The anxiety builds

In those first few months of my Jake's life, I was so anxious that I would ring Pauline or the doctor almost constantly every day, even when I still lived at home with mum and dad.

I don't remember much about the years that Jake was growing up, probably because life just carried on as normal as it could be or the electric shock treatment I had later has caused some memory loss. Pauline would baby sit every Friday so that me and Mark could go out and I looked after her two when she went out.

Out in town one morning, with the baby in his pram, a young woman stopped me, looked in the pram and asked how the baby was doing. I had never met the woman before so asked who she was. She said that she knew Mark so she knew we had a baby together. We chatted for a while and I said she should come up to the house for a brew sometime, seeing as she knew Mark. Would I ever fucking learn!

She showed up and knocked on the door. Mark looked out of the window and shouted ,"what the fuck is she doing here". I thought he would be happy to see a friend but instead he opened the door, barged past her without saying anything to her, and went to the pub! That didn't stop her coming in and even though I kept apologising for Mark's rudeness, we seemed to get on ok. Oh Susan…….

Diane, not her real name, began coming to the house two or three times a week. She played nicely with the baby but always wore revealing tops and short skirts. She had a nice figure but did she really need to flaunt it! She would lie on the floor watching telly, made herself right at home! She even babysat for us when we went for a night out with another couple to Blackpool. I have no idea why I allowed her to be there but Mark seemed to enjoy her presence, of course he did.

It was only when Mark offered to walk her home one night that my suspicions became real. I'd offered to get her a taxi but he insisted she didn't live far away. He was ages, much longer than it should have taken to walk a few blocks. I sniffed his jacket and could smell Diane's perfume. I felt angry with myself for being so stupid again, so easily taken in by this woman who was after my partner. Of course, she wasn't my friend, she just led me to think she was and I was daft enough to believe it.

When I smelt her perfume, I was boiling with rage but had the sense not to let it out because of what Mark might do. I was scared of him.

Diane continued to call up at the house. One morning she told me that Mark had asked her to go to bed with him. When he got in from work I wanted to confront him but was too scared. About a week later, Diane was in the pub when we walked in. Mark completely blanked her but she was having none of that. She accosted him at the bar and said that I had asked her if she had slept with Mark, turning the thing on its' head!

I left the pub after a few drinks to get back to Jake who was being looked after by Pauline. When Mark came in after midnight he shouted at me, saying that I was mental, then began smashing everything he could his hands on. All I could think of was Jake's birthday which was the next day.

I led in bed, once again listening to the commotion below.

For the umpteenth time I took the baby and returned to my mum's house, where I stayed for five days. I tossed and turned each night, trying to work out how I could leave Mark. One thing was blindingly obvious, I needed a bloody job.

Diane rang while I was at my mum's and told me that she would be moving into my house! I told her to fuck off, that Mark didn't want her and what a bitch she was for pretending to be my friend when all she wanted was to seduce him. Someone else rang from the pub, telling me that Mark was in a right state, sobbing and crying into his pint. He had told everyone that Diane was a slag and he wasn't interested, he just wanted me.

I eventually did go back to him again but had finally woken up to what I was dealing with, an alcoholic druggie who was a serial womaniser. I must've loved him though surely, or why did I keep going back! I still kept thinking that I needed to do something but had no idea what. I was stuck with him.

I continued to sniff his jacket whenever he had been out without me, which was still most evenings. For the first few weeks everything was fine, but then the cycle kicked in yet again.

I bumped into an old friend in town soon after moving back in with Mark that time. She asked what was up, as I didn't look too good. I told her a bit about my situation and how I barely managed on the fiver a week that Mark gave me. She said she would see if she could get me an interview where she worked, making sterile swabs for the hospital, and she was true to her word. I was shaking with nerves when I went in to see her boss, but at least I didn't pee on their carpet!

I got the job and my life began to change almost instantly. It was miraculous. I knew of a neighbour who was a child minder so I asked her to look after Jake on the days I would be working. Mark wasn't happy but by then I wouldn't have allowed him to stop me going to work.

Working on that job was one of the best times of my life. I enjoyed the work but enjoyed the friendships and camaraderie of the other women much more. I wasn't alone anymore and neither did I have to ask Mark for money because I was earning my own.

Mark continued spending his time out, all dressed up in the clothes he spent his money on. Him and his mates would regularly go to Ireland for a mega booze-up. I was never asked if I minded, just told he was going. When I planned to go to my work's Christmas party though it was a different matter.

Pauline had offered to babysit Jake at her house so that I could go to the do. Mark watched me iron the top I had planned to wear and said that I couldn't wear that as it made me look like a fucking slag – well he would know what a slag looks like, wouldn't he….. He grabbed the top and put it in the kitchen sink and poured water all over it. I put another top on, got the one out of the sink, went to the laundrette to dry it, and went to the party from there. This new defiance was dangerous.

I had spent my life with Mark walking on eggshells, trying to keep him calm, but I was getting so fed up with it. As anyone else who has been in that situation will tell you, it's bloody exhausting.

Jake also learned as he got older, that he had to be very careful around his dad or else he managed to spoil everything, whether it was Christmas, birthdays, Easter, whatever.

I know Mark's behaviour was probably typical of a lot of working class men of that era, but it was gradually becoming outdated and women had begun to stand up to it. I was a bit behind, a bit slower than the rest as Pauline would say!

Mark's drinking pals would regularly show up at the house. They'd drink themselves into oblivion, smoking weed and messing up the house. When Mark came up to bed after one such evening, I decided I could not face sharing the bed with him so got up, intending to sleep on the settee.

One of his mates was still downstairs, pissed as a fart. He lunged at me, trying to kiss me, but was easily pushed off. He apologised, saying he was stoned. I made him leave. I was finally beginning to get some confidence because I needed to protect my baby and myself!

I felt very uncomfortable whenever they all turned up any time after that. Mark had the nerve to accuse me of being dishonest and that I was going out behind his back, seen out with people he didn't know, and he was hearing about it from others instead of me. It wasn't true of course but I just could not win could I.

We continued to go out to the pub together at least once a week when Pauline would look after Jake. On one occasion I noticed that the land lady behind the bar seemed surprised to see me. She was all over Mark, offering him pints on the house. I had gone to sit at a table and when Mark returned, he was followed by the land lady with the drinks on a tray. As she passed, she kicked me on the ankle. It was so obviously deliberate. Mark called her a fucking cow, asking why she had kicked me. He threw his pint all over her curtains and we left. I knew there was probably something going on, he was back to his old ways and sure enough, it turned out he was having a fling with the landlady's daughter.

Our whole social life focussed around that one outing to the pub every week. We would get a fish supper on the way home. One night he said that the fish had made him feel sick. He paced up and down, his anger growing by the second. He said he was going to throw a brick though the chippy window. I found out the next day that he had thrown a brick but not through the chippy window, but through the off-license next door. Always had to prove he was the big man, no-one got anything over on him, or so he liked to think!

Life with Mark

Without the drink and drugs Mark was very shy. He was lovely but couldn't cope without the alcohol to give him the confidence he lacked. His parents and I would ask each other why he did it, but neither of us ever knew. It reached a stage where Mark was taking vodka to work in a plain bottle. Him and a mate would smoke a bit of weed and drink the vodka on their dinner break. He had a really good job at British Aerospace. I can't remember whether he left or if he was sacked, but what a waste.

It got to a point where he had bottles hidden all around the house, in the toilet cistern, in the airing cupboard between towels and sheets, and inside shoes in the wardrobe. It got worse and worse until he eventually turned yellow.

He was admitted to hospital but I wasn't allowed in to see him because he was having seizures and looked a mess. When I did eventually get in to see him, his eyes were black, sunken in and his lips were cut to shreds where he had bitten them. He was pacing round and round in circles. He was taken to the mental health ward because he had a history of overdosing.

He had a big scar on his tummy from a time he had tried to kill himself when he was quite young.

He stayed in hospital for a few weeks but Jake and I came home one day to find the front door open and Mark sat in the living room, staring into space. He was wearing a hospital gown. He didn't respond when I spoke to him but then began throwing things at us.

I was terrified and didn't want Jake to see his Dad like that so we ran, leaving Mark alone in the house. I went to the nearest 'phone box and rang for the ambulance. A large black van came and two men in white coats took him back to the ward that he was not meant to have left.

When Mark was eventually returned home, he looked really well, like he was brand new! He was fully detoxed. The yellow eyes and skin caused by jaundice had gone. He was quiet and loving but I remained on edge, wondering how long it would last. Not fucking long was the answer.

He lasted about two weeks and then began drinking again. If he couldn't get his hands on any alcohol, he would drink whole bottles of cough mixture but obviously it never gave him the effect he got from the booze. He began to make home brew from anything he could find.

He worked on a little vegetable patch in the garden, growing potatoes and tomatoes. I do remember once picking the potatoes quite late at night with Mark, we boiled them and ate them, sat at the kitchen table, laughing together about nothing in particular. Those potatoes were the best I ever tasted. Maybe that was a taste of how things might have been had he not been an alcoholic and drug user.

The bad memories are always stronger than the good of course, but we did have some good times together and without Mark, I would never have had my Jake.

A wedding!

I was stood ironing in the kitchen one day, when Mark asked me to marry him. I was so shocked. I held the hissing iron poised in mid-air for what seemed like an eternity. Jake was five so we had been together a long time. Why now though, I still wonder. I was so terrified of him that I said yes, even though inside my head a voice was screaming say NO!!!

Surprisingly, nobody tried to talk me out of marrying him. One friend made us a wedding cake and the rest of us chipped in towards the buffet that was our wedding breakfast.

The guest list was restricted due to Mark having slept with half of the women around Blackburn, or ex-mates who had dealt with him when he was in a drunken rage.

I only have one photo of Mark from our wedding day but sadly, none of me. I wore a cream suit and red high heels which matched a red clutch bag I held under my arm. Pauline gave me away as my Dad had refused to attend. I still have no idea why, and my mum went to the wrong registry office! Talk about having your negative feelings reinforced! Jake looked so cute in his little suit. He asked me if I would marry him too!

There was no money for a honeymoon. Life went back to the usual routine. Gradually Mark was drinking more and more. He promised he wouldn't drink too much but he had moved onto strong cider which helped him get to the state he wanted to be in much quicker than beer did.

His parents couldn't believe he had started again. He told them they got on his nerves so they washed their hands of him. His problems possibly did go back to something in his childhood but they didn't have any idea what it was and I certainly never did. It was never up to me to comment on his relationship with his parents, then or now.

Once again Mark was admitted to hospital, completely yellow. The doctor told me that they didn't offer liver transplants to alcoholics, confirming what I had suspected for so many years, that he was an addict and couldn't live without the booze. All of his mates were drinkers, the pub was his world. I just wasn't enough for him.

I was warned by the doctor that the situation was now dire, and Mark was unlikely to make it through that first night because his body was in such a poor state. Against all the odds though he recovered again, returning home detoxed and looking good, and promising to stay that way.

It lasted barely a month, maybe not even that long. Mark would pick Jake up from school but then one day, because he was too pissed to stay awake after an afternoon in the pub, he put him in our bed with him. He had been to the school drunk.

When I got home from work, I got Jake out of our bed and sent him out to play with his friends. I went down the road to the lady who used to mind Jake when he was younger, and she agreed that she would take him to school in the morning, pick him up and look after him until I got home from work.

I removed Mark from that equation to make my life slightly less stressful, and to protect Jake. He continued to be cared for by the same childminder until he moved up to high school at the age of eleven.

Jake remembers very little about his Dad other than the violence. He would whizz Jake against the wall, once throwing him across the table. He remembers him hitting him a lot but I would always try to intervene, pulling him off Jake.

I began to find evidence that Mark was playing away, yet again. I found some knickers in the washing machine that weren't mine, and a lovely ring on the floor by the bed. I put it on, definitely wasn't mine, but I made sure that Mark saw it on my finger. He said nothing but I know he saw it. I pawned it for twenty quid! It felt only fair after what he was doing, no fucking thought for me when he was in our bed with someone else while I was out at work.

On one of my birthdays, when I was 32 I think, I went into the pub where I knew Mark would be. The landlady behind the bar looked very uncomfortable when she saw me walk in. Of course, everyone in the pub knew that I was Mark's wife. There was a pint and a separate half on Mark's table. His face when he saw me told me everything I needed to know, again!

He told me to sit down while he got me a drink but then said he had to just nip out for a minute, obviously to divert whoever he had been with before I showed up.

I left before he came back, went to collect Jake, went home and calmly began making the tea. He arrived home soon after and must have been shitting it, wondering what I was going to say to him. Nothing, I said nothing…. I suppose in one way I was building up my courage, biding my time. I knew what usually happened when I stood up to him and it wasn't good.

Over and over, I thought that I couldn't allow my son to carry on living in this environment. I played it safe by not saying anything to him. Mark later took us out to the pub, a different pub, and we drank champagne for my birthday. My head was a fucking mess, and not just because of the alcohol.

Jake was growing up now he was at school, and I was able to carry on working. Once again I heard rumours and knew that Mark was having numerous affairs. He eventually left me for one of the women, who we will call Josie. He was shagging her before we got together, and apparently for long after as well.

I left work early one day because Jake's school had rung to say he was ill and I had to collect him. We came round the corner onto our street, to see Mark loading his belongings into his Dad's van.

I sent Jake indoors where he was sick in the toilet. Mark told me straight that he was leaving me. I told his Dad to take the stuff back in the house but he said Mark was moving in with Josie. So, it must have been her knickers I found in my wash basket…..bloody charming.

Mark came round to see Jake a few days later with Josie, as bold as brass. She told me that her and Mark would be really happy together. I said tell me how happy you are when he is drunk, stoned and abusing you. I said I was really happy that he was not living with me anymore and she was welcome to my nightmare.

Josie had a son the same age as Jake so they would play together when Jake went to visit his Dad. One day he came home and asked me if his daddy was also the other boy's daddy. Until very recently, I've never known the truth. I feel a bit like everybody in Blackburn knew the truth except me, and wasn't it staring me in the face and I just denied it?

We had known Josie for a long time. I had been round to see her when her baby was born shortly after Jake, to offer congratulations. I did remember her looking very uncomfy as her mum let me into the house. Her mum said, "Don't you go upsetting Susan, Josie".

I had no idea what she was on about. Josie had been seeing another man before getting pregnant but unbeknown to me, she had also been seeing Mark. I began to put two and two together but just couldn't bear the thought so buried it, as I did with so many thoughts and feelings. One of my friends at the time, did say that they thought Josie's baby belonged to Mark.

To add to my suspicions, I found out much later on, that Josie received a regular monthly sum of money from Mark's mum. More evidence no doubt, that he was Mark's flesh and blood if she was sending him money. When she died, my ex father-in-law apparently immediately stopped the payment.

They lived together for about a year, although Mark continued to be a regular visitor at my house, which was technically still his of course. While Mark and Josie would regularly visit together, Mark would also come on his own.

On one occasion he asked to take me out to the pub, even asked Pauline if she would babysit, but she was heavily pregnant and knackered, so refused.

Another time he had come on his own but Josie came following him to the door. He asked her what the fuck she was doing there and she said the same to him. He told her he had come to see his son, although it was during the day when Jake was at school! He told Josie she could fuck off. I invited her in and offered her a brew!

I don't think I knew what the word surreal meant at the time, but yes, that was definitely the feeling. I thought it was funny because I could see exactly where their relationship was heading!!

After the year of living together, Mark was clearly getting fed up and had reverted back to his nasty ways, not towards me but to Josie. It was a very weird set up. As she eventually left my house that day I laughed as I called after her "Don't worry, I'll send him back".

I had started divorce proceedings when Mark left me for Josie. I had stopped Jake going to stay at her house because Mark's boozing and drug use was escalating again, and I heard that Jake had been seen holding his dad up in the street because he was too drunk or stoned to stand up. Jake was seven.

Just a week after the divorce was due to be finalised, Mark came round to the house one afternoon. I had not seen him for a while. He stayed for his tea and sat at the kitchen table chatting with our son. He begged to stay the night, saying that he had wanted to be with me, it had always been me – yeah right. He had brought some cans of Mild, my favourite drink. He said that if Josie turned up at the door, I should smack her on the nose from him and tell her he didn't want to see her ever again.

I could see Mark was extremely ill. He looked so rough, and his stomach was swollen, not because of fat but looked weirdly tight swollen, a strange shape. I agreed he could stay, because I felt so sorry for him being in such a state. We talked all night, him telling me how much he loved me and always had. There was none of the nastiness that had characterised his behaviour in recent years. He slept in my bed with me that night, but I had told him no funny business.

He slept with his arm round me all night and I remembered the good times when we were first together and how much I had loved him. The next morning, I left him asleep in my bed. He had asked if he could come for his tea again but I told him only if he was sober. I hid his coat so that Jake had no idea he had been in our house.

When we came back after work, Jake spotted Mark further up the street, leaning against a wall. I sent Jake indoors. I walked up to Mark and told him he couldn't come for tea because he was clearly drunk again, and by that point was sliding down the wall. I helped him up and as I watched him walk up the road, he tripped and fell. When I got to him his eyes were rolling back in his head. I ran to the 'phone box to ring for an ambulance. Jake had run out after me and saw his dad on the ground. As we sat with him, holding his head, the ambulance seemed to take forever to get to us.

Mark was taken to the local hospital but was transferred to Preston neurology unit because he had suffered a brain haemorrhage. When he got there, he was put on a ventilator. His stomach was full of fluid, abnormally swollen because of excessive drug and alcohol abuse.

His mum had the horrible job of agreeing to turn off Mark's life support a few days later, once the doctors had established that he was brain-dead. The divorce had been finalised only a week or so by then and so his mum was his next of kin rather than me. I remember it was April 1st, and Grand National day. What a waste of a life, not even 40 years old.

Even if it's awful to think, I am so glad that he didn't die in my bed. I felt that I had been protected from something even worse than had actually happened.

Yet again death was at my door and I didn't know which way to turn. Having to look after Jake probably kept me going for a while, but I know I was in a trance like state, going through the motions of everyday life on auto pilot.

Of course, my mum went to see Mark in his open coffin even though I didn't. She came back gushing about how handsome he looked in his suit, which once again I thought was just weird. She seemed almost pleased, excited even, at seeing him laid out, like she got some thrill from it. I'd witnessed her in that aroused state so many times, as if she got such a kick from seeing dead people which is just weird.

I eventually went to the cemetery to put flowers on Mark's grave, only to find Josie sat there. I felt a sudden overwhelming rage towards her. I took the flowers off her that she was holding, threw them on the floor and stamped on them, grinding them into the path.

She stood up and shouted at me that there was something she could tell me that would really hurt me. I pushed her back down onto the bench. Again, so obvious, but I continued to refuse to entertain the thought that her son was also Mark's.

When we were writing this book, I talked about my belief that Mark had had a son with Josie. It was still niggling me after all those years. I was told that it was time for it to be sorted, so Jake actually asked Josie straight. She flatly denied that her son is Mark's son, but you can't blame me for putting all of those bits together and convincing myself that it was true. And I'm still not totally convinced if I'm honest.

The Police paid me a visit that evening and told me not to hit Josie again – I didn't hit her, I pushed her. One of the officers did tell me on the quiet, that they were never away from Josie's house, so he kind of understood what had happened!

Had the divorce been finalised only a week later than it was, I would have still been Mark's next of kin and would have inherited his house. Instead, his family tried to evict me and Jake, very quickly after Mark's death. I had never felt good enough for his family, and here was my proof that I was right!

They were quite well off so not sure what the rush was to sell the house. They actually came to visit on the day of their son's funeral, I thought they were there to see Jake, though heaven knows why, as they'd never really bothered with him before. They were there to tell me to get out of the house as it belonged to Mark, so they were selling it.

I decided I was going nowhere because this was Jake's home. I applied for a mortgage and much to my surprise, I got one! I had to borrow the deposit of £150 from a very good friend of mine, Billy. I invited him round for tea but was terrified of knowing how to pluck up the courage to ask him for a loan. In the end Jake told him I had invited him so I could ask him for money! I could have throttled him at that moment but Billy just laughed and agreed to the loan, bloody brilliant. My luck was changing!

A portion of the sale money was put into an account for Jake and his grandparents would occasionally give him a small amount. He didn't receive any sort of regular financial support in recognition of being Mark's son, but he did have a lovely relationship with his grandad.

He would go to their house for his tea but always felt that his gran couldn't get rid of him quick enough once he'd eaten. Jake remained close to his grandad after his gran died, and they had a really good relationship. He left Jake a considerable amount of money which helped him to get established in his early twenties which was so good.

Death, death and more death

Not that long after Mark's death, it was my mum's turn to go. She was diagnosed with cancer in her pancreas and bowel duct, but not until it was too late to treat.

I'm not sure if she hadn't had any symptoms or if she had just ignored them. She would never have talked to me about anything either way. When Pauline and I went to see her, she had lost her ability to talk and was bright yellow. I held her hand, kissed her cheek and told her I loved her. She was unconscious by then but I hope she knew I was there and that I did love her. She was nursed in the hospice until she died.

Considering how many funerals she had attended during her lifetime, hers was a very quiet affair which I'm sure she would have been disappointed with. There was no doubt that she would have been angry that we didn't have her at home, in an open coffin! We had agreed that it wasn't right to do that when she looked so awful. The short service was held at the funeral parlour because she had never been religious.

All of us were there, with my Dad. All of mums' brothers and sisters were there too, including the one who had fancied the vicar at my brother's funeral. There was so much unresolved stuff in my relationship with my mum, and now it was too late, she was gone.

I never felt that she loved me, she never showed any interest in me or Jake. She had pictures of other family members hung on the walls but none of me.

Pauline thinks that my mum thought I was alright, independent, could look after myself and that's why she didn't pay much attention to me. I craved her love and attention though, until the day she died, and if I'm honest, it left a hole, an unfulfilled need that still exists in me now.

My dad didn't last too long after his Margaret died, only a year or two at most. I still don't know if they were married at that stage, but if they were they must have done it on the quiet with none of us there! He wasn't able to manage at home on his own. He could no longer walk and had to use a wheelchair to get around. I arranged for him to move into an old folks' home. He took his budgie with him but it didn't like it there and upped and died! My dad rang me and said that even his bloody budgie had died on him!

The staff at the care home loved my dad. They were all upset when he had to go into hospital. He had spent Christmas with me and Jake, even though it was a struggle getting him to the toilet. I had a good relationship with my dad by then and still feel proud of the way I looked after him.

He told me to come and sit down for a minute with him as he wanted to tell me something. A million possible thoughts ran through my head in that moment, but I was not prepared at all for when he told me I was a bloody good mother, and he loved me loads. I was so choked up with emotion.

That was possibly the most outpouring of love I had ever had from either of my parents. He clearly loved Jake too.

When Dad was taken into the hospital, it was only a short time later that I got a call to say I should go to the hospital straight away, but before I could go, my brother rang to say Dad had died.

As I was the one who had looked after him, I took it upon myself to arrange Dad's funeral. He had told me he wanted to be cremated but my brother and sister said he should be buried in with our mum and brother. My sister all but took over, so I gave her all the paperwork and told her to just get on with it but she refused! I was going to let them both get on with it, but in the end, it fell to me anyway.

My dad had left a bit of money as an inheritance and had said it all had to go to me because I had looked after him in his final years. I couldn't do that so shared it between the three of us as I didn't understand why he had said that at all. My siblings and I rarely saw each other after our Dad died, not that we were ever close to start with.

The downward spiral

At this point in my life, I had experienced three more significant deaths in a relatively short space of time. My husband, my mum and then my dad, and of course my brother and baby Jonathan before that. My GP prescribed Prozac, an anti-depressant which really seemed to help lift my mood at the start.

After a few weeks I thought I was better so told Pauline I was not going to take the drugs anymore. She begged me not to do that, telling me that it was the tablets making me feel better, and of course she was right!

Even just one of these stressful, heartbreaking life events I had faced would be enough to tip many people over the edge. The accumulation of so much pain in such a short space of time, completely broke my mind. I had barely come to terms with the loss of my brother and my baby, and now I was a widow and an adult orphan.

I literally became a zombie, unable to cope, and I had what might be called a nervous breakdown. My son was growing up. I was no longer functioning and I eventually got sacked from my job making surgical swabs because of my poor timekeeping. That was when I got a job in a care home but I couldn't get myself together and organised enough to get to work on time.

I started going to see the GP almost every day. I was having more and more panic attacks. The GP gave me an inhaler to help my breathing. I felt I was being fobbed off all of the time by anyone I spoke to. Friends began falling out with me, except for Pauline. She paid for me to see a hypnotist to see if he could find out what was bothering me so much, but it didn't work. Maybe he realised that by then I was beyond his help.

When Jake became a teenager, he began swearing at me, not listening and was extremely hard work. He probably wasn't any different to any other teenage lad but it was me, I couldn't cope. He would answer me back and be cheeky and I didn't know what to do. I could barely cope with myself, my grief and just trying to get through each day, without having to look after him as well.

The poor lad would have been grieving too, having lost his dad and his grandparents in such a short space of time, but I doubt I had any head space to even consider that.

I know most kids go through the teenage behaviours and most parents cope even if it is unpleasant at times, but I was a nervous wreck by then, unable to cope with anything out of the ordinary. Looking back, I feel so sorry for Jake having to witness all of that, having lost his Dad, and then seeing his mum losing her mind!

There is no way on this earth that I would still be alive if it wasn't for Pauline, the best mate anyone could ever have, and that's a bloody understatement! She insisted that she was taking me to see the doctor but for some reason, the doctor came to me at home, I don't remember why, probably because I refused to go.

Events in my memory are all a bit muddled from that time on because my mind was completely broken. The doctor admitted me to the mental hospital for a few weeks, saying I had depression and anxiety but nothing seems to have come of it because I certainly didn't get better!

Around that same time, I kept ringing for an ambulance, repeatedly saying I was having severe headaches. I thought I had a brain tumour or my brain was bleeding. Nobody could ever find anything physically wrong with me.

I know now that they were psychosomatic symptoms, emotional or psychological stress showing itself as physical symptoms, but all I knew then was that I was in a lot of pain. A CT head scan showed "nothing of concern". Somehow that, and being brought home by the Police a few times, led to me being admitted to a psychiatric ward in early 2000, for an assessment.

I was scared of being admitted to the mad house but weirdly relieved at the same time because I thought that finally, somebody might get my head sorted out for me and get rid of the constant pain.

I could not think. It was as if my mind had completely shut down so that I couldn't think about anything at all.

On the ward, staff told me I had to go to daily relaxation classes, but I was *non-compliant*, a word loved by mental health staff considering how often they wrote it in notes about me! It is a polite way of saying I wouldn't do as I was told.......

According to the nursing notes from that time, I *"remained pre-occupied with physical symptoms, repeatedly saying she had a lot of pressure in her head. She said that she had something wrong with her brain, that it was dead"*.

I repeatedly asked for a scan but was refused, because I'd already had one, and all they kept saying was that my symptoms were all due to anxiety. How could it be bloody anxiety when my head felt so bad, I knew it was something physical, not fucking anxiety, why wouldn't they listen! *I knew I must have something wrong with my brain and would not be persuaded otherwise.*

I couldn't think straight but my head was full of that one idea, that there was something very, very wrong with me. Pauline had noticed that my mental state was always worse when I was pre-menstrual but of course, none of the medics picked up on that. By the age of 41, I was probably peri-menopausal which may also have caused the hot sweats I was having.

After being discharged home from the hospital on that occasion, I attended an outpatient appointment and told the psychiatrist I didn't feel any better, and that I still had bad pressure in my head. I was convinced I had brain damage but instead of helping me they sent me back to the mental ward.

The only thing I clearly recall from that period of my life, was a feeling of being so, so ill, but no one believing me. Obviously, the reason why all the scans and tests came back clear was because there actually *was* nothing physically wrong with me. My mental health notes from that year repeatedly said I had anxiety.

There's nothing much in the NHS notes between my dad dying and when I was referred to mental health services. I had been having problems on and off with anxiety and depression since the 1980s, when I was first in contact with the mental health people after I lost my baby, Jonathan.

I believe now, that because none of the root problems were identified and dealt with, my symptoms got worse and worse over time, like a festering ulcer. Of course, I didn't have a fucking clue what was wrong with me, I just knew I felt very ill and I wasn't able to cope with anything. I was labelled as *non-compliant and difficult* from those earliest admissions. It's interesting to see how this initial attitude towards me developed through my notes as time went on.

In May 2000 I was 40 and back home again and a community psychiatrist visited me to assess my mental state, and to offer advice to the community mental health team (CMHT) on how to "manage" me. According to the notes, I told him that I did not feel depressed but I was a very unhappy person. I told the doctor that since my husband and both parents died, one after the other, in a short space of time, I hadn't been able to cry. Surely the clue was there!!

I know there were probably discussions that took place between staff that I wasn't privy to, but I often wonder why nobody ever really took much notice of the fact that I had experienced the deaths of so many people close to me, in such a short space of time. Surely that would have been flagged up as significant?!

The psychiatrist did refer to it in his letter to the CMHT, but it was as if that had happened and it was over with now, of no significance! I don't want to criticise the mental health services or any individual at all, but I just wonder if I was "labelled" at the start and because of that, they missed the bleedin' obvious, or failed to focus on it. Psychiatrists tend to focus on medication to reduce symptoms whereas psychologists are the ones who look at the root of the illness, what caused it.

The psychiatrist summarised his advice in a letter to the CMHT. *"Following her great losses, she suffered a bout of depression and Prozac seemed to help her at that time. There was a period when she was without medication and remained relatively symptom free.. She had seen the CMHT Occupational Therapist and had benefitted from a behavioural therapy approach in the past."*

The OT was asked to provide some anxiety management and relaxation. Mrs Kelly is very tense, anxious and mildly depressed. Ruminates about her past and remains preoccupied with her breathing problems and occasional panic attacks. Advised to stop Prozac and take Mirtazapine (anti-depressants). All symptoms are anxiety-based. Attention seeking. Enjoys playing the "sick role".

The sick role is when somebody enjoys the attention they get and the way they are excused from doing things because they are ill. They try to make that carry on even when they are better, by pretending they still have symptoms, even when they don't know that's what they are doing.

I believe such comments about me, made so early on in my mental health journey, had a profound influence on how staff viewed me from then on, rather than looking at the trauma I had suffered of having lost so many loved ones. I can guarantee that there was nothing about any of it that I enjoyed

I saw another psychiatrist in July that year, for a follow-up appointment. I complained of being scared of everything, feeling that I couldn't cope, fear of dying, fear of having a fit, fear of losing my job. I was on sick leave by then and was convinced that I would lose my job because of the length of time I had been off sick and of course, I was right.

In August 2000, aged 41, I was admitted to the psychiatric ward again, for another assessment. All of my medications were stopped and I was referred for daily relaxation classes, but once again I was non-compliant. I was preoccupied with physical symptoms, "a lot of pressure in my head", "I've something wrong with my brain, it's dead".

The majority of daily entries in my hospital notes for this period, state that I was focussed on physical health problems. That was what I was experiencing though! I was having intense headaches, aches and pains all over my body and my head was just mush. There was no room in there for anything else.

I asked again and again for a CT scan but was refused every time, adding to my distress. Yet again, ward staff told me that all of my physical pain was due to anxiety, which I still did not believe! How could I when the pain felt so real? I knew they were fobbing me off, lying to me, but I felt powerless.

"Refused to accept that her symptoms are anxiety related, wants a brain scan. Complained of headache, back ache and pains in her legs, difficulty passing urine. Examined by physician, NAD (no abnormality detected). Somatisation. Poor sleep pattern then refusing to get up before 11am. Diagnosis depression".

20/8/00 "Continues to complain of bad headaches, feeling nauseous. Hot sweats and trembles. Looks low in mood. Staff saying all symptoms are somatic and anxiety related. Attends to her personal care at this time."

Again, I stress that I'm not setting out to criticise anyone, but in reading through the reams of documents, letters, nursing notes and so on, it does feel as if how I was viewed as a patient was set very early on, which is scary. I hope they don't still do that now.

During that admission in August, I had a diagnosis of long-standing, free-floating anxiety, with perceived symptoms of depression. I had been prescribed two anti-depressants, but neither had made any improvement to my mood. The notes said that I had a tendency to ruminate secretly about my past, present and future. How the fuck did they know that if I was doing it secretly!!

"Psychiatrist wanted to admit her to QPH for further assessment and proper diagnostic formulation to make it easier for her to understand her problems and also for the purpose of her future management in the community."

Future management makes it sound as if I was The Problem, which I suppose I was!

When my medications were changed again, to see if they would improve matters, it was documented that I was feeling hopeless, helpless and worthless with guilt. Staff attributed the feelings to no longer being on Prozac.

"Denied suicidal intent – has a fear of dying. Admitted to ward for assessment while being taken off all meds.

Wants to be like her old self. Feels worthless because she can't care for her son.

23/8/00 Wanted to go home and attend day services due to problems with Jake and needing to find alternative accommodation for them both. Went to stay in a guest house but failed to return to the ward for the ward round".

I was discharged home again in September, in my absence, because I didn't go back to the ward when I was meant to. The only support I had was an outpatient appointment which I did go to, and I told the doctor, yet again, that I didn't feel any better and still had bad pressure in my head. I remember being convinced I had brain damage but none of the bastards believed me.

My diagnosis seemed to change about as often as I changed my knickers. When I went to that out-patient appointment I was given the diagnosis of anxiety neurosis with hypochondriacal ideas!

My memory of this part of my life is very hazy. Pauline and Jake can fill in a lot of the gaps, but the next part of my story relies heavily on my NHS notes.

7/11/00 Referral to psychiatry from A&E. Susan stabbed herself with a kitchen knife. Psychiatrist stated that while an in-patient previously, she was assessed as having behavioural problems rather than a depressive disorder. Advised GP to refer Susan for a neurological check and CT scan for her hypochondriacal symptoms – finally!

Jake and I continued to live in the house that was originally Mark's. Jake had said to Pauline that he wasn't sure he wanted to live with me anymore but she encouraged him to stay. Maybe she thought he could keep an eye on me. He gave me my medications every morning before he went to school.

These days he would be called a young carer but there was nobody other than Pauline knew about the situation the time. Jake was happy to give me the pills because he knew that they kept me well.

What he didn't know for a long time was that I was secreting them under my tongue and spitting them out as soon as he turned away. Jake stayed over at various mates houses more and more because I was telling him that I was immortal, that I couldn't die and he just didn't know what to do with that.

In November 2000 Pauline contacted the mental health crisis team rather than my doctor. She was so worried because my mental health had deteriorated over the past few weeks and she didn't know what to do. She didn't know about me not taking the pills.

I'd been picked up by the Police while wandering the streets of Darwen at night. What the fuck was I doing out at night when I had a teenage son at home! I hadn't a clue where I was going or what I was doing. The Police picked me up and took me home and the day after, was when Pauline contacted the mental health. At the end of November, I was admitted to the psychiatric ward again.

Jake eventually went to live with Pauline. She just took him in, there was never any question in her mind about him going into formal foster care or anything, she just accepted him as if he was her responsibility.

How bloody amazing is that, especially when she had her own family to look after. She is an absolute queen amongst friends. She didn't get any money for looking after him, but she continued to care for him throughout the years I was in hospital. It upset me when he later went to her with his problems rather than me, but I can fully understand why! I was hardly the mother of the year back then.

Once again, I denied any mental health problems but said I was fed up with people saying my problems were all due to anxiety. I said I couldn't sleep, eat or drink and hadn't done for two weeks. I said that was due to *the thing* growing inside me. I said to them that it was highly contagious and it was stopping me from leaving the house because I didn't want it to spread to other people.

When I was asked what I thought the solution would be, I wondered how they could be so fucking dumb with all of their bloody degrees and training. Why couldn't they see that I needed to have *the thing* surgically removed and replaced with good organs and a new head? All they could talk about was mental fucking health!

The "thing" was something new that I had not mentioned before. Reading it now, it's as if my problems were getting worse because I wasn't just complaining of headaches, I actually thought that I had a "thing" living inside me. I was delusional.

In November 2000, there were no psychiatric beds available at Blackburn, and I was taken to the John Elliot Unit in Rochdale. They could have taken me to Mars for all I knew or cared. When I was transferred back to Blackburn in December 2000, the discharge letter stated, *"She complained of having creatures inside herself and had funny sensations in her brain.*

It felt as if her brain had swollen up inside her skull. She said that the creature inside her had spread through her body. She felt that she was dead and living in a shell.

She repeatedly requested a scan in order to confirm and check the creatures inside her.

She admitted to having a death wish but denied any plans or intentions of harming herself. She had tried to stab herself a few weeks previously in the abdomen. She was trying to get the fluid out of her body. Her intestines felt blocked up. She felt that she had already died and at other times she said that she was never going to die."

I really don't have any clear memory of that time, but what is obvious is that I was becoming more and more of a fruit loop. Yes, I know, before anyone complains about my lack of political correctness, fruit loop is not a nice thing to say about people with a mental illness, but I am only referring to myself, not generalising.

By then the *"thing"* had developed into *"creatures",* so I was getting worse.

I told the doctors at Rochdale that I had my first breakdown years ago around about 1980, soon after the time of my brother's death but didn't have any psychiatric help at that time.

Before I was transferred back to Blackburn, I had been put on section 3 (s3) of the Mental Health Act, which two doctors and a social worker had assessed me for. It is a treatment order and can last for up to six months.

I don't remember being assessed or told I was detained or that I could appeal against the decision, but I would have been told at the time. I was no longer allowed to leave the hospital without permission from a psychiatrist.

In January 2001, I was discharged home. I refused any support from the community mental health team. I clearly wasn't ready for discharge because by the end of the month a neighbour, concerned about my mental state and behaviour, had contacted the bloody mental health team.

An Occupational Therapist visited the same day and found *"Susan agitated, pacing, pressured speech, emotional, and outbursts of anger and aggression. Susan made reference to stuff entering her body through her legs and entering her stomach. Neighbours reported she was lying in the road in front of travelling vehicles putting herself and others in danger. She had failed to attend an assessment for daycare services at the hospital. Reluctant to respond to questions. OT contacted psychiatrist who agreed to admission for assessment and treatment."*

I was admitted to the mental ward again. Apparently, I became difficult to manage on the ward. She reported *"feeling dead, with aliens living inside my body parts. She became obsessed with her tongue, subsequently biting into it and causing a lot of pain. She set fire to a bin in her bedroom and was highlighted as a fire risk. Sent on home leave and then refused to return to ward."*

Yet another Mental Health Act assessment was carried out but I wasn't detained that time. I agreed to return to the ward as a voluntary patient once arrangements were made for Jake's care. That was January 2001. Jake was 15. He had been spending more and more time sleeping at his mates, but eventually he went to stay with Pauline.

When I returned to the ward, the notes say that my personal hygiene had deteriorated, I was not communicating, was not motivated and had no interest in anything.

I apparently weighed 12 stones at that time, but by August 2002 that had increased to 16 stones, and by November 2006 I was 17 stones and 4lbs. My diet was clearly not good, or it was possibly side effects of medication that caused the weight gain. I weigh much less now, in 2024, and take a lot more care with my diet and exercise because I now have type 2 diabetes and chronic obstructive pulmonary disease, COPD.

While on the ward in August 2001, I was reported to the Police as missing. A risk assessment completed a few days before, had highlighted areas of concern because I still believed I was immortal, and evil. I had said that I wanted to kill someone in the hospital, or weirdly, a priest in a cathedral. I had also said that I was going to set myself on fire.

They must have got me back to the ward because the notes stated a few days later that I was lying on the floor in the smoke room, saying I had a fly growing inside me and had demanded a full body scan. I then stood up and ran off, saying I was going to throw myself under a train.

There's a section of the Mental Health Act that can be used by nurses in emergencies, to stop patients from absconding from a ward, section 5(4), was used to detain me because they thought I was at risk of killing myself. I was assessed and detained under section 3 again, in September. It seems as if I was just getting worse and worse.

My diagnosis had changed again to one of treatment-resistant psychotic depression. The psychotic bit means that I had delusional beliefs about being immortal and having things growing inside me. I tried to set fire to the bin in the manager's office again in September and for that, I was transferred to the PICU, the psychiatric intensive care unit, the ward where the most dangerous, volatile, and difficult to manage patients are held. I would love to know why I was trying to set fire to a bin! What was going on in my head!

Quite by chance at some point in my hospital journey, my own house set on fire due to a faulty kettle – nothing to do with me as I wasn't even there! The insurance company made all the arrangements to have repairs done but it meant whenever I was on home leave, I had to stay in a bed and breakfast until they found me a flat.

Pauline and Jake continued to visit me in hospital but I wouldn't talk to them so Jake eventually stopped coming. He felt he had no connection with me anyway and it was if I wasn't there. My poor lad.

Pauline would buy me new clothes, underwear etc but they would all go missing so she had to stop doing that in the end because it was costing such a lot of money!

Nothing seems to have changed much by the end of that year. The psychiatrist explored my ideas with me, that I was dead inside. Staff were recommending that I would need to go for rehabilitation before I could be allowed out into the community and "real" life.

I was rude to staff, threatening towards them, and trying to damage property on the ward. The Occupational Therapist wrote that I *was, and had been, a difficult lady to manage, both in hospital and the community.*

I couldn't put my feelings into words that anyone understood. No matter what, I was being injected with anti-psychotic drugs by then to try to get rid of my delusional beliefs. The doctors believed that the things I kept saying about being immortal and evil, were delusional beliefs that needed to be treated. Delusions are fixed beliefs that can be part of a severe mental illness.

The doctor had suggested that I might benefit from ECT, Electro Convulsive Therapy, which sounded terrifying to me. It was referred to as shock treatment. I had heard from other patients that it was a short electric shock through the brain. That's what it actually is, but it's safely done under anaesthetic, in a controlled way, by a doctor trained to do it. An electric shock is passed through the brain and that induces a fit or seizure. It can affect the memory but very often it will reset the brain so that the depression goes away. It sounds brutal but it does work for most people – not me though…..

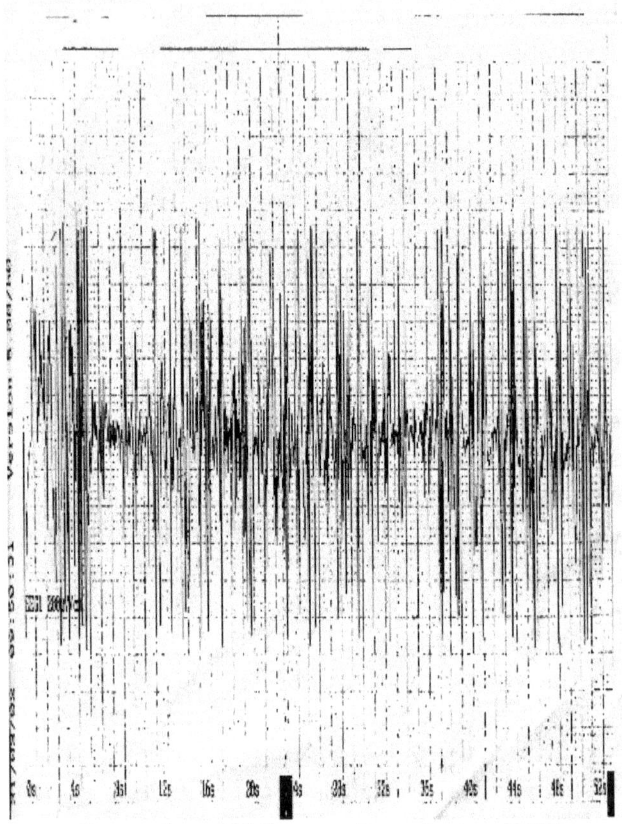

Part of my EEG recording during ECT

I'd had yet another change to medication at that time and whether it was that or my dread of having ECT, I began to try a bit harder. *"Susan is attending to her hygiene and makes herself presentable. She has struck up a friendship with a male patient on another ward. This appears to have helped her mood and motivation as she has a purpose."*

I'm still friends with Paul to this day and we've been a big help to each other. When we were in hospital, I thought Paul was my angel. He was the only person that ever smiled at me in the smoke room and I thought he had come to save me. We ended up in the same rehab unit years later. We seemed to follow each other round from ward to ward, hospital to hospital. We would go to the cinema together. I once got him a bottle of vodka but the nurse in charge poured it down the sink!

Like everything else, the improvement didn't last long. In December my notes state that the OT and nursing staff thought that I was sabotaging any plans to discharge me. When I was made to go on leave, I did nothing in my own home, but at Pauline's I cooked and did all sorts! I told staff that I had problems with my cooker so didn't want to cook there but I'm not sure that was the real reasons – I didn't want to be left on my own.

It is documented a number of times in my hospital notes that I wanted to re-establish a relationship with my son Jake. That's not how he remembers it though. He says that on one occasion, probably later on, he visited me while I was on home leave. There was a box of cereal on the table and without a word, I picked it up and slowly poured it all out on the table. I then picked each little piece up, one by one, and flicked it at my son.

He says that initially he laughed but that just seemed to make things worse and when he asked what I was doing, I stood up, grabbed a large knife and chased him with it. He ran upstairs and shouted out of the window for help. The Police came and took me back to the ward, again.

Knowing how much I love Jake now, I can't imagine why I would have done those things to him, unless it was part of the way that the illness showed itself. I am so lucky that he has turned out to be the man he is and that he sees no point in dwelling on the past.

I continued to make attempts at sabotaging my leave but it was unsuccessful because they had worked out that was what I was doing.

Back on the ward again at the end of December, I lashed out at staff when my lighter was removed during the night. I was restrained and yet again I was flat on my face on the floor.

In January 2002, aged 42, I was sent on home leave but had to return when ECT treatment started. The sessions were four days apart. At ward round I was still presenting as quite distressed, crying, and saying I was immortal. I also said that I felt sorry for my son, having a mother like me. My leave was cancelled.

Mid-February I was *"still unstable, expressing thoughts of self-harm, harm to others, destruction of the ward and equipment, refusing meds as said they don't work. In tears when seen in ward round and repeatedly saying she is immortal and born with no feelings."*

Cigarettes and smoking seem to have been a particular trigger point between me and staff. I'd been told to remain on the ward due to my aggressive behaviour after being caught smoking in the dining room when my cigs and lighter were confiscated.

Never one to do as I'm told, I waited until staff were bringing the dinner trolley in and then sneaked out of the open door. I was eventually found on another ward where I was verbally aggressive with staff when told to go back to the female ward. I apparently said I am not a child, don't treat me like one, although my behaviours suggest otherwise don't you think!

At that point I must have still been detained on a section because there is a copy of the Psychiatrist's report in my notes for a Tribunal. I must have appealed against my ongoing incarceration.

"Susan had been under my care for over 12 months for the treatment of her chronic depression. There is no apparent diurnal variation in her mood but she has persistently expressed ideas of delusional intensity in that she is convinced that she is immortal and even if she is run over by a car whilst crossing the road she will live. This is an unshakeable belief which is very worrying.

She also believes that her stomach is full of aliens and maggots. She claims that she was born with no feelings, no emotions, and no amount of argument can convince her otherwise.

Her response to anti-depressants has been partial. She has been given 12 ECTs with partial response with regards to the lifting of her depression any apparent improvements have been short lived. We have already asked for a second opinion from Forensic Consultant psychiatrist. His response is awaited."

So, I was institutionalised, with a diagnosis of chronic depression but elsewhere it says that I was to have increasing periods of leave, both escorted and unescorted to my home address and I could have unescorted leave to the local shops.

Then I was moved to the PICU again, because I still had outbursts of physical and verbal aggression and still thought I was immortal. Seems to be lots of anger on my part, and anger that is not addressed, can turn inwards into depression.

Time and again throughout 2002, I would be restrained. I began to hide medication, was I planning an overdose? If I refused my injection of medication, I would be restrained and injected while lying on the floor. I could be held for what felt like hours sometimes, until I calmed down.

I told one nurse that I would take one of their swipe cards to get off the ward so I could throw myself under a train or bus. I was desperate to prove to them that I was immortal and they needed to believe me!

I'd said that it was terrible that staff didn't understand that I had no feelings and there was nobody else in the world like that. My mood seems to have been getting lower and lower. Pauline continued to visit but felt that there was no connection with me anymore. Most people would have given up on me by that point.

Reading all of this I feel really, really sad and upset at how ill I was, but also that it feels as if I was already being viewed as a hopeless case and a troublemaker. I can see how my behaviour could be interpreted as deliberate, but I still think it was a cry for help when I couldn't voice how I was feeling or why, because it was still too painful to deal with.

"It seems that Susan has become very dependent on services in the hospital, despite her not accepting that she has a mental illness.

Her range of difficulties have caused exasperation amongst those caring for her and I am impressed with the tenacity with which she has been treated, despite a disheartening ly poor response".

I have found all of that very upsetting, reading how the nurses and other ward staff had struggled to look after me because I was so difficult and horrible towards them. I must have felt very isolated and alone, if I was feeling anything at all, but I can't remember. I can't remember anything!

The person I am now, I can't believe I was ever so horrible to people trying to help me get better. I don't think I have an ounce of bloody aggression in me now!

The psychiatrist from the secure hospital seems to have done a very thorough assessment but she didn't offer me a place, because I wasn't bad enough to move there. Probably a good thing…

"Her current clinical presentation and the general nature of the risks she poses and her treatment needs would place her so low down the waiting list for the secure unit, that it would be unfeasible."

When the doctor discussed using anti-psychotic medication, she said she was going to suggest trying another medication called Clozapine because I wasn't getting any better no matter what they tried. Clozapine is an anti-psychotic medication usually used to treat schizophrenia. I told her I couldn't care less what they tried. I was so depressed I didn't care about anything.

She also told me about the benefits of psychological therapy. If I had had access to that, it may have been the key to a much earlier recovery and was a disappointing, missed opportunity due to lack of resources. How sad.

As is often the case, everything comes down to cost, money and lack of resources. Or maybe the psychiatrists disagreed on how useful psychology might have been at that time, who knows.

I'm sure a psychologist would have picked up on my belief that I was a living corpse and linked it to my repeated experiences of death. Surely the bizarre experiences of mum taking me with her to visit corpses laid out in their coffins, must have had a link to how my mental breakdown presented itself in my delusional beliefs. Looking for a cause might have been better for me than treating my symptoms. It does seem that is what I was occasionally trying to say.

24 July 2002 " Susan became very tearful while in smoking room. Discussed various life events with nurse, including when Stephen died, she remembered not being able to express her feelings and became angry. Unable to explain why she felt angry. Questioned herself why she was like that. Susan believed that she had murdered her husband. She said she drove him to drink and take heroin. She said she didn't love him when he proposed marriage but married him because he asked and she was scared to say no.

During the marriage he had an affair. She now feels she is being punished for all she done wrong in the past. She said her mum would have told her to pull herself together. She also said that if her mum was still alive, she would have to murder her".

It's so interesting to read what I was saying. Things were so mixed up in my brain.

Suddenly at the beginning of August, after the assessment by a Forensic Psychiatrist, I was saying I had feelings again! I said that I did actually love Jake. I would have a daily shower, change and wash my clothes. I said I would not demand cigarettes from other patients and I would take all my prescribed medications. I wanted to go on a diet and have my make up.

What was going on?! I even apologised to staff for being so un-cooperative and then tidied my room! I thought the doctors would change their minds about sending me to a secure unit, if I did everything they always asking me to do. I even said that I was mortal again and that all of my feelings had come back. What I didn't realise was that I was going anyway, even if not to a secure unit!

None of it lasted long of course, because it must have been so hard for me to maintain such a lie. I still really believed that I was born with no feelings and that I was immortal. As that was my fixed belief, anything else was a lie.

I was soon demanding cigarettes from staff followed by threats to throw plates or to hit someone. C&R was used yet again. *"Susan has relapsed, expressing delusional ideas of being immortal and having no feelings and all her organs are dead inside"*.

There are records of odd times when I did seem able to speak honestly to staff and I would ask for 1:1 time with a mental health nurse. One wrote in my notes that *"she is immortal and has no feelings since she was born but went on to say it was 3 years ago when her body felt unusual and began to lose all her feelings. She asked the nurse why she felt like that and how she could get rid of the negative thoughts. Susan said non-one could help her as no-one understands her and they aren't willing either."*

Other patients began to complain about how bad I smelt. I told them I didn't need to wash because I was immortal. A care plan dated 5/9/02 states that if I didn't attend to my own needs, staff would take control to ensure that I did attend to my hygiene.

And that is exactly what they did. They dragged me into the shower and were in there with me to ensure that I was washed until I was squeaky clean – how humiliating, but all very legal.

The staff's plan was discussed with the Mental Health Act administrator at the hospital, to ensure that they would be acting legally by having 1:1 staff in the shower with me to ensure I washed properly!!

The administrator spoke with the NHS Trust solicitor. It was found that due to the ward environment and the welfare of other patients, staff can take such drastic action when dealing with a patient's personal hygiene.

The shock of being washed by someone else must have had quite the effect on me! A day or so later, I began having showers and washing my hair without even being told. I didn't want to be in hospital or be moved to secure or have anyone in the shower with me ever again. I had even, unbelievably, joined in conversation with staff about my previous jobs. *"Susan said she used to make wedding dresses, shoes and jeans. She became quite animated telling a tale of when she worked in a factory."*

Unbeknown to me though, I wasn't going to a secure unit but I had been accepted by a low secure rehabilitation unit in Warrington. So, my good behaviour plan had failed.

From that point I had nothing to lose with my transfer planned for the end of October, so I began to refuse medication again. I was angry, sullen and said I wasn't going anywhere. I repeatedly told staff to piss off.

I must have been off the ward at some point because a male patient told staff that we had been *"engaging in sexual activity."* When asked about it, I asked what they meant, the wanking? Staff apparently counselled me about consequences of my behaviour – I would love to be able to remember what the hell they meant by that!!

When the time came in October 2002, for me to be transferred, there was a formal discussion between staff as to whether the patient, me, should be sedated prior to being transferred by ambulance to Warrington. They decided I would be given an injection of Lorazepam if I became verbally or physically aggressive towards staff, and that three C&R trained staff would go with me in the ambulance. Human equivalent of a strait jacket!

I just can't put myself in the place now, where I can imagine that I was such a bloody threat to anyone, but they clearly thought I was at that time.

After two months, I had started to settle down on the new ward. Seems I eventually started to engage with activities, including working with their Occupational Therapist. My delusional beliefs were still there and I remained a fire risk because I continued to smoke in bed.

I was aggressive. My sleep was very poor. I refused medication and isolated myself in my bed area. Same old, same old.

I was referred to psychology and actually began to engage with them, but then stopped. Maybe I still wasn't ready to be able to deal with facing my feelings and the things that had happened to me.

The lack of response to the treatments suggests to me now, that they were missing something – would you agree? Or maybe I was still too ill to take part.

There should have been a way to encourage me to talk about my experience of death, the deaths of people close to me but also my regular visits with my mum to view dead people I didn't know.

Pauline visited me but I didn't have any contact with Jake at all during that period. Pauline decided there wasn't much point carrying on coming all that way to see me when I was unresponsive. She told me to ring her if I needed anything and apparently I did once, and she began to hope that this was a sign I would recover, but of course it wasn't.

While in the unit I was allegedly responsible for five incidents of arson, including setting fire to the patient storeroom in the hospital. I still don't believe I did that and certainly don't remember if I ever did!

According to the hospital notes, the clinical team noticed an improvement in my mental state which they said was down to medication. I had been prescribed an anti-psychotic called Clozaril as recommended by the Forensic psychiatrist. I was still deluded about being immortal and having no feelings, but had apparently been easier to engage, more communicative, less verbally aggressive and with much prompting and support from staff, I would even tend to my hygiene.

Even though my psychotic symptoms remained, I was more compliant, most likely because Clozaril mixed with all the other meds I was taking, can do that to people…

By June 2003 I was still improving! I was reported to be pleasant and co-operative and caused no management problems! I must have been a lot less smelly because I was having a bath most days, but still needed encouragement to change my clothes, even though I had bought new ones. I'd even had a haircut and my overall appearance was much better apparently!

It's really encouraging to see how well I was doing in that unit! I was joining in with most activities. I particularly enjoyed the cooking and went out to the shops, escorted by an OT, to buy ingredients. I was accepting medication.

As a reward and recognition of my compliance with everything staff wanted me to do, I was given six hours of unescorted ground leave which I reportedly used appropriately, meaning I probably didn't try to escape. I was only allowed into the hospital grounds, but that must have felt good, to be outdoors on my own, to sit smoking. I have absolutely no memory of my time at that unit, or of how well I did.

In July 2003 Jake turned 18 and was having a party. I'd not had any contact with him for ages. I didn't really have any clothes to go out in, but I wanted to be at Jake's party – I was his mum! I had a brown top that I wore, what I mess I looked, so fat as well.

Jake's 18th

Staff escorted me to the party otherwise I wouldn't have been allowed to go. There were lots of people there that I knew but I don't remember speaking to anyone. I do remember Jake being really upset when I had to go back to the hospital, and I cried all the way back. My poor boy, seeing his mum in such a state, and being escorted like a prisoner. I bet there were a few tongues wagging once I left!

Jake had returned to live in our old house when he was 16. To this day he believes that the house was haunted, which of course would have thrilled my mum had she still been alive. She would have arranged for an exorcism!

Unexplained things regularly happened, noises, bumps, and Jake would see a man out of the corner of his eye or walking across the top of the stairs. Years later Emily, his daughter, would see someone in the house when she was very young, and Jake even caught something on camera when he took a picture of how distressed Emily was.

In September 2003, the doctor's plan was for me to continue with psychology, continue with anti-psychotic and anti-depressant medication and I was to be encouraged to rebuild relationships with Jake and Pauline who had stopped visiting me a while ago, believing that I was no longer interested in her friendship. I was also to be granted escorted home leave, working towards unescorted home leave. I was to have a support worker to help with domestic skills and further integration back into the community.

It seems as if I was doing very well, doesn't it! I could have been discharged home at that point and lived happily ever after but something must have gone wrong somewhere around that time because sadly, of course, that is not what happened.

In October 2003 I appealed against my detention to a Metal Health Tribunal, as was my legal right. Needless to say, I didn't get off the section and had to stay in hospital. I wonder if that had a really negative effect on my recovery and caused me to relapse, thinking I was never going to get out. My deterioration was rapid. It seems I had completely given up.

Just over a year later, I was moved to a place in Blackburn because I was no longer getting any benefit from being in the low secure unit, which was a very expensive placement. The Council were paying a lot of money for me to be there and seeing no improvement. Feels to me that I was still very unstable. I would seem to do well for a while but then relapse due to the slightest little upset.

The discharge letter from Warrington, dated November 2004, gave my diagnosis as severe depression, chronic anxiety with a delusional thought disorder and paranoid schizophrenia – bleedin' hat trick!

"Continues to believe that she was born with no feelings and is immortal but is no longer suicidal.

Feels that meds are doing nothing for her.

It also said that I was losing my teeth due to neglect.

I must have still owned the house in Darwen that had originally belonged to Mark. I had got a mortgage to pay his siblings their share when he died, so that Jake and I could remain in our home. Due to being in hospital for so long I had not paid the mortgage and was £19k in arrears. The building society had put the matter in the hands of a solicitor.

Jake was only 19 and didn't want his name on my mortgage because he would have then been liable for the arrears. After a rethink though, he got his own mortgage and bought the house from me, with most of the proceeds that would've been mine, being swallowed up by the arrears. I wanted to give the remaining money to Jake to help him refurbish the house. That's when it got complicated with a bloody social worker doing their best to interfere. I know they were only looking out for me but still……

The solicitor involved in the sale was concerned that I lacked the mental capacity to understand what was involved. They wanted to be certain that I understood what it meant to sell my house as I would technically become homeless.

To have capacity I had to be able to understand the information, retain or remember it long enough to weigh up my options and then communicate my decision to the solicitor. Seems I was able to do that!

What really bothered them though, was me wanting to give some of my proceeds back to Jake so he could get jobs done on the house. The social worker asked if the sale could be put on hold while my capacity was tested again. Jake was so very angry at that and I was so, so mad at the social worker and typically told her in no uncertain terms.

I was given a new care co-ordinator/social worker soon after and eventually I was able to give some of my money back to Jake for work on the house although he said he didn't need it.

I wasn't able to stay with Jake while the refurbishments were happening. Jake had also said to staff that he wasn't sure he could cope if I went to live with him. We were not close at all and I must have seemed like a stranger to him, a stranger who still said weird things.

6/2/06 "Susan seems to have finally accepted that she cannot go to live at Jake's and she will have to find rented accommodation. She is reluctant to look for properties in the paper, or to make any decisions and continues to revert to the born with no feelings state. She uses that to shut down conversations about housing etc".

I wasn't very happy at being moved back to Blackburn and when I arrived I refused to get out of the taxi. When they did eventually get me indoors, I refused a full physical and blood tests. I spent lots of time on my own on my bed. I said that I didn't think I would ever get better.

The Occupational Therapist wrote,

"Susan lacks motivation and the responsibility to participate in many of the activities of daily living skills. With encouragement and prompting, Susan will independently function in many of these areas."

What a sorry state of affairs for a 45 year old woman to be in. I missed out on so much life, and all those years of Jake growing up. I cannot remember a single thing about that part of my life. I must have been so, so poorly, my mind completely broken. For all that time I spent in hospital, it seems that nobody was able to reach me while I was so locked into the state I was in, even when I occasionally did try to open up to someone. Maybe there was something inside that knew I needed to talk.

"1:1 time with a nurse talking about looking after alcoholic father, losing Jonathan at 21, blamed mother for having no emotions. Felt unable to grieve for baby or brother. Born without feelings, but then said it started 4 years ago. Nurse pointed out she was weeping therefore must have feelings. She dismissed that, saying her life is empty.

I remained adamant in my denial about the fire setting. I even rang someone who I believed had set me up, and it was really them who had started the various fires. Nobody believed me because I always had a lighter when I wasn't supposed to and I would fall asleep with a lit cig in my hand so always had burn holes in my clothes.

Time dragged on through the next few years in much the same way it had for the previous ones. Staff had concerns that my ongoing hospitalisation might increase institutionalised and dependent behaviour. Yet I would remain in hospital for another five years.

I was moved around to a few places but nowhere could manage me. I was taken back to the hospital ward.

According to my notes, I was very unhappy with the series of quick changes. As a further change, I was being encouraged to think about moving into residential care as a long term option. That's a massive thing.

It meant that there was never any hope of me getting any better than I was at that point.

Back on the ward I spent much of my time led on the settee or in the smoke room. I still refused to wash or change my clothes, didn't see the point. My hair was bedraggled and hung around my face.

I paced the corridors, barely speaking, not really communicating with anyone. If someone tried to speak to me, I would tell them that I was a living corpse or that I had been born with no feelings and refused to engage with them.

I would stay on the ward until a residential or nursing home would take me.

Poor Jake had had enough and in 2005 said that he wanted to get on with his own life and wanted nothing more to do with me. He was in a settled relationship with Leanne by then. I was a lost cause. …..

23/5/05 Ward round. "Awaiting funding for residential care. Remains unmotivated, pushes boundaries. No attempt to contact Jake. She said again about no feelings and that she hated her mum and dad. Felt guilty for the past and what she has put Jake through. Susan in agreement to go to residential care".

I was 45 years old.

Staff felt that I might have some underlying personality issues. I think they were working their way through a list of possible diagnoses to see which fitted me the best. *"She can be manipulative and resourceful at times when she really wants something. She requires extensive prompting to motivate herself to self-care. Personal hygiene remains very poor. Continuing incidents of disinhibition and sometimes she doesn't dress properly and her breasts are exposed."*

About this time, I was made to go out once a week with a support worker, who reported that I was always unkempt and dishevelled. However, I did seem to be a bit more communicative with her than with others. On one occasion I bought a bunch of roses for a staff member who was leaving. The support worker asked why and I said I liked the member of staff so wanted to give her something as she was leaving. The support worker, who I think was called Sandy, challenged me about not having any feelings as buying roses contradicted that.

I shut down and refused to discuss it any further. I wonder if I just didn't understand what I felt or it was too difficult being challenged to face up to the fact that I actually did have feelings.

When the funding was eventually agreed for residential care at the end of 2005, I refused to go!

The current social worker told me I still had to go and to start looking in the local newspaper for properties to rent. I didn't, because I was totally disinterested.

25 March *"Susan has arranged to view two flats in Darwen. One needed a jolly good clean. Susan had to pay a deposit but she deviously tried to manoeuvre events to avoid paying a deposit. Nurse arranged for letting agency to come to ward to collect the deposit which Susan was not happy about. She said she had changed her mind and wanted to house share with another patient. One flat likely to be ready in a few days as landlord was asked to clean it up."*

Deviously seems a hard, judgemental word!

The consultant agreed *"a month would be permitted to secure the tenancy, and discharge arrangements would be confirmed at next ward round. She could have leave at the new flat.*

At this point I was being given an ultimatum that I was being discharged and would be made to leave the ward as I was no longer responding to treatment – had I ever?

5 April "Meeting with social worker. He emphasised the need for Susan to secure a tenancy asap as she is no longer gaining any benefit from being in hospital. He promised that that there is a great deal that can be done to improve her quality of life and to help her access services and facilities in the community.

She then said that she was born with no feelings and therefore believes that there is no point in doing anything. The social worker reminded her that she had believed that for some time but still needs to live her life. She said that she cannot get any pleasure from anything.

At the end of the meeting Susan told the social worker that she is planning to discontinue her medication as she thinks this does not do anything for her. Social Worker strongly encouraged her not to do that.

I was reported to be settled mentally, really? Yet I continued to lack motivation re personal care, and my room was a mess. I was repeatedly turning down accommodation that I thought wasn't suitable. Maybe I didn't want to go?!

The psychiatrist also told me I was no longer gaining any benefit from hospital provision and I would probably just become even more lethargic and deskilled the longer I stayed in hospital. I said they couldn't be make me leave if I had nowhere to go. I was told to accept a property even if it is not what I initially wanted or I would end up in a hostel. |At that point, I regretted selling the house to Jake.

By mid-May everything was in place for me to move off the ward. The doctor had said I couldn't go to a hostel as I wouldn't cope and it had to be a tenancy. The flats I'd seen had fallen through but I found a house in Darwen that I really liked. It says in my notes that I would need a lot of support to establish domestic routines but then goes on to say that the social worker would visit once a week – so I was going from being observed 24/7 to a once a week visit.......

The support worker was to remain involved, to advise and encourage me to live a healthy lifestyle and to access local social and leisure activities as appropriate.

I went to the bank for the deposit for this house. I would eventually get housing benefit towards the cost of the rent. With the money in my bag, I went to meet the landlord at the property. I would go on leave from the ward for a week and be visited by the social worker during that time.

When I went on leave, I left my Clozaril medication on the ward. Deliberate? Clozaril is the type of anti-psychotic medication that has to be re-titrated, or restarted, all over again from the starting dose if you stop taking it. So, the social worker brought it to me, of course they did.

Jake had contacted the social worker to express his concerns again, about me not being able to manage in a house. He believed that I would sabotage the situation in order to get back into hospital. *"She had said to Jake that she might get nasty and show us i.e. staff.* When the medication was dropped off, I said I wouldn't take it.

What was I doing.

According to the notes I was pleased with the house I had found to rent so why was I trying to sabotage my leave already. Part of me thinks that I must have felt terrified to be back out in the world, mainly on my own.

There seemed to be a difference of opinions in how I was coping during the first few days in my rented house. The social worker said that the house, was well equipped. I had arranged to have the 'phone line reconnected. I even took the Clozaril and Fluoxetine while he was there, and he congratulated me for doing so well in securing such a nice property. I had said I was happy with it and I still knew a lot of people in Darwen. His notes said that I was unable to tolerate him for long and began to pace the room saying I had no feelings.

The mental health crisis team had been made aware of me being on leave for the weekend and I had been given relevant numbers to contact if anything went wrong.

Jake saw things in a much more realistic way than the social worker. He rang and said that I had *"displayed some alarming behaviours when visiting his house and he is no longer going to allow her into his home as his girlfriend gets very upset by Susan."*

"Susan soiled herself on their settee and then tried to strangle herself in front of Jake's girlfriend. Susan later denied that this had happened. She is constantly ringing Jake asking him to go round to hers. He had given Susan his old mobile. The social worker felt it was all attention seeking behaviour."

What the fuck was I playing at doing such horrible things to my son! It sounds at that point that the social worker was right and this was disgusting attention seeking behaviour but what did I expect or hope to gain from it!! I seriously don't get it!

Probably the saddest part of this whole story is my relationship with my son Jake. As I said earlier, my best friend Pauline took Jake to live with her without a second thought because he was only a young teen when I was first admitted to hospital.

According to the hospital notes, our relationship had broken down because of my behaviours. I find it so disturbing to read about it as I just can't remember, and I can't imagine ever treating him that way. He had found it very difficult to cope with me whenever I was on home visits.

Jake had expressed concerns to staff about my relapse pattern when I had previously been discharged from hospital. He said that I had posed a significant risk to myself and others when unwell in the community.

"He was concerned that in the past it had been left to him to manage supporting her with her needs and feels she needs support from mental health services on discharge"

"She would intimidate him and his friends for money and cigarettes, calling on neighbours and others on the street for money and cigs in her nightclothes during the evening. She refused to go to bed and slept on the sofa, refused to do anything for herself."

Was I still very ill or just idle? I had no motivation to do anything. Was I still grieving or was I experiencing the effects of unresolved grief, many times over? I wonder if I ever grieved in a natural, healthy way for any of the people I had lost. I clearly had an unhealthy relationship with death because of my mum and her interest in seeing dead people.

Many of Jake's mates remembered me from when they were younger and when they would come for their tea after school. They must have been frightened of the person they saw I had become.

It wasn't unusual for Jake to come to the house I had rented and find it full of local kids. They were using it as a doss but I wanted to keep them sweet because they would go to the shop for my fags. He got rid of them.

On another occasion he came to the house to find I was stood on the bedroom windowsill, naked from the waist up, moving slowly from one foot to the other, staring at nothing. I refused to come down to open the door, wouldn't even recognise that he was there in the street below.

Jake rang for the Police and when they arrived one of them found an open window that he was able to get through. I had come downstairs at that point and was pacing around and around in circles.

The young Police officer was obviously scared of a half-naked mad woman, as he frantically searched for the key to the front door!! Jake laughs when remembering that particular incident because of how terrified the policeman seemed to be!

Needless to say, that was another free ride in a cop car for me, back to the ward, but was almost immediately sent back on leave because they thought I needed to stick with the plan!

Jake doesn't dwell on the past and considering the mess both of his parents were, he has come out of it really well. He is happy that we have the relationship that we have now and sees no point in going over all of the bad stuff of the past. He's even able to laugh about a lot of it now!

The hospital had been told that I needed to be discharged almost six months earlier so it is no surprise that after another week's leave I was formally discharged. I didn't bother going up to the ward round, I couldn't see any point in wasting my money on a taxi. They must have had a party to celebrate finally getting rid of me!

I was sent a copy of my discharge care plan, a very important document apparently. *"Susan has a history of severe depression and anxiety and this is accompanied by a delusional disorder. She has now been discharged after a very long hospital admission. She can become very distressed and preoccupied with concerns that she has no feelings.*

In the event of Susan having any concerns re any of the above she can contact the following......care co, crisis team, GP or go to A&E. The expected outcome would be for Susan to receive prompt and effective assistance in the event of a mental health crisis".

I'm not sure who was meant to be watching me for these signs of relapse because I'm sure that *I* wouldn't be able to tell that I was relapsing!

Maybe Pauline and Jake were expected to watch me and tell the mental health people if things were going wrong.

The first few days post-discharge are recognised by mental health professionals to be the riskiest in terms of relapse or self-harm, for patients who have been discharged from a psychiatric ward. At the time, the guidance said that the care co-ordinator had to see the patient within seven days of discharge but it has since been changed to within 48 hours as the risk is known to be highest during those first few hours.

When the social worker came to check up on me the front door was wide open, and I was there, sat in the lounge, almost where they had left me. *"Initially appropriate but presentation quickly changed, became tearful and expressed some distress that she had no feelings and could neither live nor die. Began to pace around the room and was slightly hostile as she asserted that I could not understand how she felt."*

She said that she wouldn't die if she jumped under a bus and briefly put her hands to her throat. She said she was lonely and begged me not to leave. She said she liked me and wished she could be like me.

Confirmed she had food in but not eating much. Said she didn't like the house. Attempted to discuss care plan with her but her presentation prohibited that."

He wrote that much of my behaviour was attention seeking as I managed to regain my composure several times.

The social worker went back and discussed me with the psychiatrist who again said that I needed to consider residential care if the current situation broke down altogether. No immediate recall to the ward on that occasion.

Things did break down very quickly of course, and I managed to stay free for less than two weeks. When the support worker came round I wouldn't let her in. She could see me through the letterbox and I told her to fuck off because I didn't want to see anyone. I did ring her later to apologise for swearing at her and to tell her again that I was immortal, born with no feelings. I also told her that I hadn't had a bath since moving in because the water wouldn't get hot. She told me to contact the landlord to get it looked at.

I know I was meant to be independent but it still feels as if they didn't help me very much but I've probably forgotten just how much they did do for me. It's easy to criticise at this distance but I really don't want to be critical of anyone.

The social worker said they would visit me one week later but instead she tried to catch me out by coming to the house the next day. She brought some mail that had gone to the ward and a few clothes I had left behind but I'm sure it was an excuse to get to see me.

Unsurprisingly, I didn't bother going to my Clozaril appointment to get my bloods checked. Blood tests are important when you are taking Clozaril, to make sure your white blood cell count is ok as it can become too low, making you vulnerable to infection and other stuff.

The support worker came again so I hid behind the curtains. She came to the window and asked about missing my appointment. I said I knew about missing it but I wasn't bothered.

Poor Jake continued to bear the brunt of my behaviours. He rang the social worker again, expressing concerns about me. He was told to ring the Police who would break into the house because I was refusing to answer the door. Instead, he contacted Pauline and she and another friend broke into the house through the back door. I was in a right state.

"On gaining entry, Susan was animate, pacing, saying she couldn't breathe, had no feeling, could not live or die, wearing no top, staying at top of stairs and refusing to come down. Jake felt she had not been eating or drinking or taking care of herself in any way. Not taken any medication. Felt she had lost weight and some teeth were missing.

They all felt alarmed at her presentation and didn't think she had been coping at all. Susan refused to leave the premises for over 2 hours. Ambulance in attendance. Jake was eventually able to coax her out of the house, strongly asserting that his mother cannot cope in the community."

Pauline and another friend took me straight back to the ward in the car. One of the junior doctors felt intimidated by me apparently! I was dishevelled and distrustful. I lifted up my top and said look I'm not breathing. I also said that I wanted to die because at that point I really felt that I had nothing to live for.

There must have been several hearts that sank when I was seen coming through those doors back onto the ward! I agreed to be admitted as an informal patient so no need to section me that time. Was that what I had wanted all along I wonder, to be back where I felt safe, where I didn't have any responsibilities and didn't have to think?

I hadn't paid any rent in the house. The housing benefit claim hadn't had time to be processed. My care coordinator/social worker advised the landlord it was highly unlikely that I would ever return to the rented house.

He was very understanding but must have suffered a financial loss which I'm very
sorry about. He was so good about it. The tenancy was terminated. Was that not proof enough, again, that I was just not ready to be turned out into the real world!

"On the ward she remained monosyllabic, glaring at people, difficult to engage. Spending time in bed, low profile on the ward."

As an informal patient, they had no legal power to place me in a residential care home at that point even if that is what they wanted to do, and I certainly wasn't going there willingly.

When I was reviewed by the team soon after I was readmitted, they decided I was unable to cope in the community – no shit Sherlock….

"Needed rapid titration of medications. Said she was not sleeping or eating well and that she can't breathe. Self-neglect, staring, suspicious, speech minimal, relapse of psychotic illness. Re-titrate Clozaril, prn Lorazepam and Haloperidol.

Discharge planning to be resumed. All staff agree that it is unlikely she will be able to engage with Community Services sufficiently to facilitate a return to her own accommodation. Mental Health Act to be considered if she tried to leave the ward."

To this day I have no idea why I lost several teeth during that short time that I was out of hospital. It could have been a gradual build-up of neglect I suppose. It had been recorded in my notes several times about my poor dental hygiene. All I had left were several stumps sticking out of my front lower gum. I don't remember them coming out but I was in a lot of discomfort which made me not want to eat.

Daily notes say the same thing day after day after day.

June 2006 "Long periods in her room but came out for supper then went to the smoke room where she spent time talking to a Nursing Assistant. She said that she is rotting away inside and cannot cope".

In July 2006 somebody decided that I should be transferred for more rehabilitation. Other places had been asked to assess me but nothing ever seemed to come of it. It had all been tried before and everyone knew it didn't work.

23/7/06 " General consensus that Susan will not manage in her own tenancy. Continues to express delusional beliefs and while out had informed the nurse if her mother wasn't already dead she would fucking kill her anyway."

I clearly blamed my mum for some part of my illness.

13/7/06 Support worker refused to take Susan out in her car due to her smell. Staff said that she goes into the bathroom and runs the shower, but doesn't get in. Puts a towel round her head when comes out to make it look like she has washed her hair when she hasn't.

Some of the staff seemed to have a low opinion of me and some of the words used to describe me were very negative e.g, abrasive, argumentative, sullen. Probably no surprise by that stage though.

By September the support worker had withdrawn from trying to work with me due to my lack of engagement. I'm sure she worked really hard to try to encourage me to do things and she was very supportive of me, but I must have made her job extremely hard so I'm not surprised I was pulled from her caseload.

"There is currently considerable concern about the need to be planning for Susan's discharge as she has been identified as a patient who is a delayed discharge and is blocking a bed. Senior management are very concerned for these sort of patients to be discharged as soon as is practicable.

Possibility of Susan being assessed by the Women's High Dependency Service at Guild Lodge." These sort of patients………..There's a whole debate to be had just from those four words….

"Consultant expressed reservations about that as she had already spent time in a similar unit in the past without gaining any benefit. Susan to have a new Consultant who may be able to bring a new perspective on Susan's difficulties."

I told the social worker that I wanted to stay in the Blackburn and Darwen area and would like to go to sheltered housing. I had said that I felt I could manage in that environment, but apparently the nurse reminded me that I hadn't managed in my own tenancy even with support. Yeah right, cheers for that, even though I know it was true.

"Susan referred to staff seeing her as a fire risk which she has repeatedly denied. She described her attempt to cause a small fire as being of no consequence and attempted to minimise the event.

Susan expressed some low self-esteem and futility about her future saying she was useless as she was obese, depressed and neglectful of herself. She explained that none of her problems could ever be addressed as they all relate to her central is Susan of her having no feelings

Nov 2006 age 47, Susan's weight 17st 4lbs, height 5'2.5ins so morbidly obese. Encouraged to be more active on the ward. Printed information given to her but she said she wasn't interested. Poor diet on ward but orders take away or goes to KFC."

There was a Kentucky Fried Chicken outlet across the road from the hospital and I would use my leave to go there, usually in a taxi. It would have taken less than ten minutes to walk.

I think from reading the notes for 2006, the staff were really fed up with me, and wanted rid of me, but every attempt to move me on would fail.

17/12/06 "Susan complains of having no feelings, being empty inside for the last 9 years"

I was still being prescribed the anti-psychotic medication Clozaril and my diagnosis was now acute psychosis. Nobody seemed to have been interested in why I said I had been like that for nine years, unless they thought it would be more of the same.

It does feel as if I had mentioned a few things that suggest to us now, that I wanted to talk about my mum and other things that had happened to make me like I was, but it was very rare that anyone actually sat and asked. I was never offered counselling of any sort.

As I've said before, I'm not criticising the staff, they were all extremely busy, always under pressure, and I must have been viewed as a right pain in the arse for most of the time. Seeing a patient on the ward for all those years, not getting any better, must be so discouraging for all of the staff.

Yet another Christmas and New Year went by. Jake says that was the only time he really missed having a mum when he was young, was seeing his mates opening presents with their mums when he had been invited to theirs for Christmas.

By February 2007 there seems to be a more decisive attempt to move me on from the ward. Medications were changed and more discussions took place about where I could go. Residential care was mentioned again, as a serious option.

The psychiatrist planned to take me off the anti-psychotic as I had not shown any benefit from taking it for such a long time. It had made me gain loads of weight. The doctor thought that once they took me off it, they would be able to tell more clearly if my "behaviours" were actually due to mental illness, or deliberate as they repeatedly said they were.

"Susan continues to voice delusional ideas, says she is a living corpse, born with no feelings. Continues to be fairly un-co-operative on the ward. Says she is depressed. Susan began to repeat that she had no feelings and was immortal."

This time when I said I was depressed, I was prescribed an anti-depressant that I had not had before, Lamotrigine.

My care co-ordinator/social worker told the ward round that *"Susan has potential but has no belief in herself or her abilities, and her condition has manifested in significant behavioural symptoms and her continued manipulation."*

He was to be responsible for arranging my accommodation for discharge this time. I was a bed blocker, because I was not gaining any benefit from being in hospital.

I was assessed again for a secure unit, though not sure why at that stage of things. Thankfully, they didn't think I was bad enough. The forensic psychiatrist though, had suggested another diagnosis, not one that had been considered before.

There's a lot of psychiatric jargon and stuff in this next bit, so feel free to skip it if you are not interested! It's part of a psychiatrist's report and provides a different perspective on my illness.

We felt that bits of the report needed to stay in as it is a really important part of my story from the mental health side of things, rather than just what I can remember. The psychiatrist had gone through all of my old notes, very thoroughly, and had written a report with some interesting observations.

"Diagnosis of residual schizophrenia. Known to services since 2000 and in hospital for several years. Her initial presentation was suggestive of a severe depressive illness and I suspect she probably had a prodromal phase before her first admission to hospital. Over the years the symptoms have been progressive and currently we are left with a largely deficit clinical picture characterised by alogia, avolition-apathy, asociality.

The positive symptoms are the unusual beliefs of being immortal, having been born with no feelings and her thoughts being taken away by her mother, which at times reach delusional intensity, but in the recent past has not been affecting her functioning as much.

The other positive symptoms include disorganised behaviour and the issues regarding fire risk are related to this. She also had an episode of catatonia when medications stopped after her transfer to Hyndburn ward earlier this year. She continues to have nihilistic delusions and a depressed, flat affect.

Diagnostically, I feel that we are looking at a case of residual schizophrenia. Her deficit state means that most of her skills are impaired. A trial of Clozapine was given in the last few years but issues relating to monitoring of bloods means that this is no longer a feasible option.

Her current medication regime is designed to try and tackle both the depressive and psychotic domains of her illness. However, what is clear is that because of the chronic deficit state she will need long term supported accommodation.

An assessment of capacity to consent to treatment done today reveals this is intact. She was able to appreciate the discussion regarding her future placement which she said she would think about. She is also able to agree that her behaviour of smoking inappropriately should not be indulged in.

Capacity is issue specific and dynamic so this would need repeated assessments over a period of time for an overall judgement call to be made regarding her capacity to decide upon the issue in question."

The overall clinical picture is therefore of a lady with some positive symptoms, and a significant number of negative symptoms with a basic, but somewhat reasonable level of insight.

The significant negative symptoms, means that the skills necessary for adequate functioning in life are significantly impaired.
I therefore support the application for appropriate long term supported accommodation."
I barely understood a word of that, but it seems everyone was of the same opinion – I had to go into residential care, probably for the rest of my life.

Things start to change

On the evening of Thursday May 3rd 2007, I was sat in the foyer of the mental health unit and saw my son Jake outside, coming towards me. He was 21 by then and had been in a relationship with Leanne for quite a while.

I was surprised to see Jake as we had not spoken for a long time, but not half as surprised as when he told me that I was a nanna! Me. A nanna! I couldn't believe what he was telling me! He said he would take me to see the baby the next day.

I went into the hospital shop and bought a card, chocolates, flowers and a balloon. When we arrived at the maternity unit though, I realised how dirty I was, my fingernails were black, and I refused to hold the baby even though Leanne said I could. I told her I was happy just looking at the baby.

My first grandchild, baby Emily, and I couldn't hold her because of the state I had allowed myself to get into. I didn't want to infect her with anything.

Those were the first real emotions I had experienced in a long, long time. I stared at the tiny baby in front of me, wondering how I would ever be able to love her when I could not even love myself.

Jake has a very different memory of that day! He says didn't come to the ward to tell me he was a Dad, because we'd had no contact for ages, and his head was full of other things!

He remembers nipping down to the shop for something, and he was shocked to see me coming along the corridor towards him, holding balloons in one hand and trying to hold my pants up with the other! We have no idea how I knew about the baby, who had told me, but I was definitely on my way to the maternity unit!

I firmly believe that Emily being born, was a pivotal moment in my recovery. I had something very special to get better for, my first grandchild.

I was overwhelmed with emotions. My son was a dad and I was a nanna, a fucking nanna!!

When I think of everything Jake experienced it would not surprise me or anyone really, if he had cut me off completely, but when Emily was born that was the start of us rebuilding our relationship. What an amazing young man.

Another significant change that happened at that time was I was given yet another care co-ordinator.

On the day that Emily was born, Sheila, who has written down my story for me, was having an interview at Darwen resource centre to become the deputy manager of the community mental health team. She got the job and we met for the first time in July 2007 when she was allocated as my latest care co-ordinator. She was 48 and I would be in the August. I have said that she saved me but she disagrees, saying it was a combination of her seeing something in me that she liked, medication changes and Emily being born. Even after Sheila discharged me several years later, we stayed in touch and eventually became good friends. And she is writing my book!

So, the stars were aligned, they say things come in threes don't they. Lamotrigine, Emily and Sheila – the three things that I believe helped me to finally get better, all happened within the first few months of 2007. Sheila picks up the next bit of the story.

Sheila

When I moved my new job at Darwen community mental health team I was allocated a small case load of patients who had severe and enduring mental illness. One of my new colleagues gave me an additional file to add to the pile on my desk. He said something to the tune of here you go, you can have this one as well, as a fresh pair of eyes are needed. He smirked as he turned away, as did a few other staff close by, as if they were all in on a joke I wasn't privy to.

I suspected this file belonged to a difficult, well know patient, and it did. It belonged to Susan Kelly. It was the first one that I read and it proved interesting! I was looking forward to meeting someone who believed they were a living corpse as I didn't think I had ever come across that as a delusional belief before! The other thing that struck me though, was Susan's date of birth, three months after my own – we were the same age.

When I eventually went to the nurses' office on the ward where Susan was a patient, I was given an overview of her mental state and the difficulties she presented on the ward. It was a priority to get her moved elsewhere, as she was not gaining anything by staying.

I said I would work with them in trying to achieve that, while inwardly rolling my eyes and wondering how I would manage that in light of the long line of professionals who had preceded me – certainly a bit of a challenge!

I was told that I would find Susan on one of the corridors as her bedroom was locked so she couldn't go in there to smoke. She wasn't hard to miss.

She looked like someone who had escaped from a Victorian asylum. She was trudging up the corridor towards me very, very slowly, a large lady with very long matted hair, barefoot, wearing a white nightdress that had food and drink stains down the front. I introduced myself to her but she looked right through me, before saying that she was a living corpse.

I told her that I was her new care co-ordinator, a social worker, and I was here to help her move to somewhere other than hospital. She repeated that she was a living corpse. Ok, good start! I walked back down the corridor with her, until we turned around and came back again. Susan said she was born with no feelings. I was unable to gain any other response from her.

I told her that I would be back for ward round at the end of the week. I tried to get her to give me some eye contact but she refused to look at me but said again that she was a living corpse.

I suppose I initially felt a bit unsure how to approach her but decided I would just keep visiting and see what happened. I imagine that most new care co-ordinator's felt that they would do their best to help her, but it was almost impossible to build a rapport with someone who would only utter the same two phrases over and over again.

The thought repeatedly returned to me that Susan is just three months younger than me. I could empathise with the depression that she had experienced, to some degree, but couldn't help thinking how different our lives had been.

I found the bits of history in her notes fascinating, but suspected that there must be much more to it.

I carried on visiting her at least once a week and we would pace the corridors each time, with her telling me she was a living corpse, born with no feelings.

Attending ward rounds, I was informed by the doctor that there was nothing else that could be done for Susan. So, I now had the job of finding her somewhere to live and it had to be residential care, where she would likely remain for the rest of her life.

I could see where he was coming from because of her history, but I was also appalled at the thought of this 48 year old being consigned to residential care! I wanted to do my best for her, as I did with all patients obviously, even if the end result for Susan would be the expected one.

As a social worker/care co-ordinator it is vital to maintain some distance between yourself and the patient. It's not advisable to become emotionally involved or attached to the patient, because of the power imbalance that inevitably exists between you. At the time I was an Approved Social Worker so, as an agent of the State, had Susan needed to be detained under the Mental Health Act again, I would have had to complete that assessment and further deprive her of her liberty, had it been appropriate to do so. That is quite some power imbalance to be aware of when trying to get to know someone.

As the weeks went by and we continued to pace the corridors of the ward, I began to gently challenge Susan whenever she said she was a living corpse. I said she didn't look too bad for a dead person. She began to look at me as if I was weird, possibly because no-one had said that to her before, who knows! I would ask about her new grandchild, about her son and her friend Pauline, but she didn't respond.

Very, very slowly, over many weeks, Susan began to engage, talking a bit more each time we met. I felt so sad that she was in the situation she was in, that she had had so many bad things happen to her that had conspired against her mental health, and eventually resulted in her having a mental breakdown.

I could not imagine having to spend so much time away from her son. There must have been something in me that saw something in her that was worth fighting for?

Not long before I met Susan, the doctor had introduced the anti-depressant Lamotrigine and she seemed to have responded well to it. I believe that was a key factor in her recovery.

Lamotrigine is a drug usually used to treat epilepsy. Susan did experience one seizure in 2006 but there was no explanation why and she has never had another one since. Lamotrigine is also used as a mood stabiliser in bi-polar disorder as well as chronic, severe depression. It could have been the combination with the other medication she was prescribed at the time, but once that Lamotrigine was introduced, there was a really positive shift in Susan's mood. Every time I saw her I felt that she was improving a little bit and I really liked her!

In a ward round in November 2007, I informed the gathered professionals that initially I had agreed with the recommendation for Susan to be transferred to residential care as a long term option. However, having spent time with her on a regular basis, I felt that she had improved significantly since the dose of Lamotrigine had recently been increased and I now felt that Susan would benefit from some time in an intensive rehabilitation setting with a view to eventually moving to supported living in the community.

Of course, because of the previous attempts at rehabilitation, and me being a newcomer to the multi-disciplinary team, I was told that was *not* a viable plan, as it had all been tried before and failed.

I was advised to look at a residential home in Rawtenstall, as a placement for Susan. I remember the Consultant Psychiatrist saying that it was considered to be the end of the road for patients who went there, but that was where Susan needed to go.

The fact that she would be transferred to the care home was now inevitable, but I was determined that was *not* where she would spend the rest of her life. I encouraged Susan to engage with the ward staff to try to improve the way she was doing things. Due to the positive changes that the anti-depressant had made to her, she was able to do that!

I told her that she had to show what she was capable of, and we came up with a list of things that she needed to be doing, including looking after herself without being told to do so!

The Consultant Psychiatrist wrote " *She is more willing to engage and has agreed to visit some prospective placements. Having been in hospital for many years she has lost most of her basic skills. She is now responding to a care plan with firm boundaries in place, and for the first time in years it appears that she may have some potential for rehabilitation. There are still many issues around how Ms Kelly became so ill and why this has not resolved, but these issues could be dealt with in an environment other than hospital.*

Obviously nothing was easy, as Susan refused to co-operate whenever she was presented with accommodation other than hospital. A care home in Rawtenstall identified as the main placement of choice at the time, but she refused to be assessed by their staff. I persuaded her that I would take her to look at the place to see what she thought.

By that time, we had an amazing support worker, Donna, who was also putting a lot of time and effort into working with Susan to help her re-learn lost skills. I felt that Susan was beginning to trust Donna and me, even though her delusional beliefs persisted. She even let Donna take her to the hairdressers because her hair was all matted. The hairdresser said there was nothing she could do but cut it all off. Donna told her there was no way and she took Susan back to the hospital. Pauline had already cut a big knot out. Various staff, bit by bit, spent time getting the knots out of her hair. She was going grey.

Susan would tell me a bit about herself, about Jake and about her childhood. The delusions that she expressed seemed to have some links to childhood, when her mum would take her to visit dead people, without giving any explanation of why, or what death was about. I thought that was one of the weirdest things I had ever heard.

From November 2007, nursing notes finally became more positive in reports about Susan, saying she was pleasant most of the time, and on occasions didn't even mention being a living corpse.

She remained compliant with the care plan. It definitely wasn't all plain sailing and Jake certainly didn't think he could see any change in his mum at that time.

The changes probably were quite small and I think poor Jake had heard it all before, and seen so many attempts to discharge his mum that had gone wrong, that he was right to remain sceptical

Even though the situation remained fragile, staff documented a positive change in Susan's presentation, that she was pleasant, and humorous! She said that a few feelings were coming back and when asked what they were she said, *"feeling tired and wanting to go back to sleep"*. Susan began laughing because she had made a joke!

"Day leave to her son's house. Came back to the ward in good humour, spontaneous in conversation, talking about her baby granddaughter, but still occasionally expressed she is a living corpse - easily diverted back to the conversation."

During the time that I had known Susan, I had never seen her wear a bra, but in talking about her goals for discharge, she had told Pauline that she wanted to get one before their 50th birthday. Pauline took her to be measured - 46DD. Susan told the lady measuring her that she was a living corpse at least twice – who knows what she thought! The next time I saw Susan I couldn't believe how different she looked just from wearing a bra, her ginormous boobs were no longer hanging over her belly!

Don't get me wrong, there was no miraculous overnight recovery for Susan. She still had days where she would stay in bed, refusing to speak or eat, but for most of the time she remained in a more positive mood. She would still say she was a living corpse or she was born with no feelings. However, she continued to attend cookery group and had demonstrated that she was a good cook.

As the time approached for Susan to visit the care home she was not quite as bright and she said she had lost her smile and wouldn't get it back. I spent time trying to reassure her that I would be with her every step of the way and we would take everything as slowly as we could. In the few months we had known each other I felt that she had begun to trust me.

Towards the end of December 2007, Donna and I managed to get Susan to visit the care home. She didn't want to go and when we got there she refused to go up the steps to the entrance. She was highly anxious, visibly shaking, and began to say that she was a living corpse.

It was obvious that she reverted back to saying that when she was anxious or uncertain about what was happening. We gave her lots of reassurance and she eventually agreed to have a look round, with us on either side of her, in case she decided to try and do a runner.

After discussions with staff beforehand, it was a huge relief to know that Susan wouldn't be expected to live in the main care home, as I felt that would be so detrimental to her mood. The other residents were mainly older adults, some with dementia and she would not have liked it.

The rehabilitation part of the care home was really nice. It was arranged into small bungalows to give the feel of some independence even though staff were around all of the time. Susan would be expected to keep her own space clean and tidy, as well as herself.

The staff were very encouraging and felt that they would be able to work on improving her skills.

Susan was fine on the way back to the ward that first time, relieved that the visit was over. She agreed to think about accepting a place at the care home, whenever one became available, although she didn't really have any other options to be honest!

There were some scary moments when I wondered if I had pushed Susan too hard. As the New Year came around she refused to get out of bed for anything or anybody.

She had spent Christmas with Jake and that had all gone really well. Staff were spending a lot of time with her trying to persuade her to get out of bed and to follow her care plan, but she was argumentative with them.

Susan and I continued to visit the care home on a regular basis, whether she liked it or not. We were getting to know some of the staff who would be involved with her and she began to talk to some of the other residents.

Plans were in place for her to move in March as it was expected that there would be a space for her by then. Some days she was adamant that she was never going, she couldn't do it, and others she could be persuaded that it was a good move.

Susan spent more and more time at the care home, eventually staying overnight. By then she rarely mentioned having no feelings or being a living corpse unless she was stressed. She was allowed leave from the care home so we would regularly go to the local Asda for bits of shopping she needed to cook for herself, and we would go for a brew in the café when I visited.

We never used the escalator when we were in Asda as Susan was too anxious, so we used the lift. I remember her ringing me many months later to tell me that she had finally used the escalator on her own! That might seem like nothing much but for her it was a massive achievement.

When the day of the discharge ward round arrived and the room was full of professionals! When I first met Susan the year before, I never envisaged getting to this point. I felt so proud of her in progressing so far, and a huge sense of relief from the ward staff!

There were obviously still those who expected the whole thing to fail. Susan had been under the care of mental health services for 24 years in total and the last eight of those had been in hospital with little or no sign of improvement. She had had plenty of failed discharges, but this time it felt different because if the rehab' bit did fail, she would remain in the care home rather than return to hospital.

Susan was so very anxious about being discharged to but recognised she could not manage on her own at that stage. Staff there said she would be assessed and provided with a full programme of activity once living there permanently.

Jake was in favour of the care home and saw it as a good move. At least he knew she would be safe there.

There was still scope for further improvement in Susan's mood following the clinical improvement with Lamotrigine, but that would be monitored.

Susan was discharged from hospital on 31 March 2008, and that would prove to be the very last time that she was in a psychiatric hospital. A momentous day!

Susan would need ongoing support as she progressed with her recovery. There was always a chance of her relapsing so I continued to see her on a regular basis and ensured that she attended her out-patient appointments with the psychiatrist.

The staff were pleased her with her slow but steady progress. She was living in her own small bungalow like unit, cooking for herself and keeping the place tidy. She was taking more care of herself and she had made some friends amongst the other residents.

Susan remembers one of the other residents putting salt in her milk for nor reason and she didn't realise until she drank it! She also remembers being able to hear another woman using her vibrator all night, every night! When she asked the woman about it she said she couldn't help being highly sexed!

Jake would come to collect Susan and take her to his house for tea. Their relationship was gradually improving. I continued to liaise with the rehab' staff until we felt that it was time to think about Susan's next steps.

I had contacted a rehab' unit in Blackburn to see if they felt Susan would be suitable for their service, which they did! Susan was very pleased at the thought of moving to Blackburn, but also highly anxious again about facing another change. She still does not like change!

Susan remembers me coming to tell her that it was time to move on and she was not happy!

As the time approached for Susan to move again, I got a telephone call telling me that she had been arrested for stealing a lip gloss in Asda. I was fuming!

I knew exactly what she was doing, trying to sabotage the move! I drove over to Rawtenstall where Susan was sat in the office, looking very sheepish. I told her that I knew what she had done but it made no difference, she was still moving! She still laughs about that now, as she says, she knew I would know exactly why she stole the lip gloss!

Apparently she had picked up a lip gloss in full view of a security man in Asda and put it in her pocket after she had paid for her shopping! She went outside to get in a taxi but the security man came after her and took her back to the manager's office. They agreed not to call the Police, but she would be banned from Asda indefinitely! The security bloke said he didn't understand why she'd paid for loads of shopping but then stolen a lip gloss! Little did he know it was a sabotage plan!

Ages after, Jake and his mate pulled a prank on Susan by ringing her and pretending they were Asda security. They said they needed a picture of my rear end to put on their criminal's board! She nearly blew a gasket before I could hear them giggling away, so knew who it was immediately and told them to piss off!!!

Susan moved to Blackburn with her belongings and despite her anxiety, quickly settled into life on the unit. She had a bit more freedom there but was still accountable to staff. She began to complain about other residents who would leave the shared kitchen in a mess and on more than one visit I would go in to find her up to her elbows in soapsuds, cleaning the kitchen.

Susan had regained much of her enjoyment in her activities from long ago, such as cooking. She got on well with the staff and after a few months we were already thinking about her moving on to somewhere where she would be living independently.

The thought of living completely independently still terrified Susan. There were very few options other than her renting a house or flat somewhere. She wanted to be as near to Jake as possible.

Susan tried to delay her move for as long as possible. Her name had been on waiting lists for one or two supported accommodation schemes but whenever we went to visit, she would find fault the place.

Eventually I got a call from the supported living scheme at in Blackburn as they had a vacancy. They specialised in providing accommodation for people with long standing mental health difficulties, while allowing them to live as independently as possible, which sounded ideal!

We met a member of staff and viewed the property. It was one of a row of terraced houses owned by the scheme.

Susan and Emily, now and then

Susan took an instant dislike to it as she felt it was too big for her. We had a good look around but there was nothing about it that would convince her it was the right place for her. When the member of staff came back to see what we thought, Susan blurted out that she would not be moving in!

The member of staff was really lovely about it. She told us that one of the flats in the main block across the road had just become available. Susan was a bit reluctant to view it but we went across the road with the staff member and went up to view the flat on the first floor. It had its own front door, one bedroom, bathroom, and combined kitchen and living area. Susan fell in love with it instantly and asked how soon she could move in! In her mind's eye she could see exactly what she could do with the place because it would be her own space. It felt right!

Things moved very quickly from there. I had to sort out funding for the tenancy. Susan had been detained under section 3 of the Mental Health Act on a couple of occasions which meant that she was entitled to section 117 aftercare. So, some of her tenancy was funded through that. I was able to secure a grant for Susan as she was leaving long term care. We enjoyed buying essentials such as a kettle, toaster, microwave and much more, because Susan had nothing to furnish a flat with. She still reminds me that I apparently bought her a full set of towels as a moving in gift!

Susan would initially be provided with support time every day. Over the years that has gradually reduced although at times it can still be very useful.

In as little as two years, Susan had progressed from being a mental hospital in-patient of more than eight years, to moving to an independent living flat.

Susan takes up the story again from here.

I do remember the day I first met Sheila when she came to a ward round. I think we liked each other from the start but I didn't make things easy for her, why would I when she was just the latest in a long line of bloody busy-body social workers! She said things to me that I don't think anyone else had and eventually I liked it!

Sheila says that it was the new anti-depressant that made the difference and becoming a Nanna, but I have always believed that she was the one who made the difference to me getting better. I'm sure the ones before her tried their best, and she says they prepared the way, but I still call her my rock. Who knows where I would be if she hadn't come along! She gets very embarrassed when I say that and says she was only doing her job!

The staff here have always been brilliant with me. Sheila carried on seeing me but gradually her visits reduced as I didn't need as much support. I was taking my medication without a problem because I knew it was keeping me well, better than I'd been for years! She would take me to my outpatient appointments with the psychiatrist and he was pleased with my progress. At the first appointment he had said to Sheila that it was inevitable that I would relapse with my history……

Life continued to improve from then on. I decorated my flat, gradually getting it just how I wanted it, regularly went to Jake's for my tea and saw Pauline as often as I could. She was glad to have her old mate back!

Jake and Leanne went on to have Leasey in 2012 and twin boys Lennox and Carson in 2020. What a different experience that was to when Emily was born. I had hold of the babies as soon as I possibly could, no longer worried that I was too dirty. I regularly babysit and they are the most important people in my life. As a Nana I have the family I never managed to achieve as a mum.

When I moved into my own place I began to take more care of my appearance, applying make-up and finally got my hair dyed. Gradually I got my love of clothes back too! There's a woman who has a stall on the local market and she recently said to me one day that I was a beautiful woman and she always loves to see what I will be wearing! She will never know what an impact that had on me, such a massive confidence boost from a stranger!

Across the first few years in my flat, I got into a good routine. I would go out into town on my own, always by taxi as I could never face going on a bus where there were lots of other people. I usually met up with Pauline or one of my other friends. I'm very lucky in having a good group of mates who I have known for a long time.

Sadly, not all friends turn out to be what I first thought they were. I was still vulnerable I suppose, still too trusting when I met a young Asian bloke who moved into one of the flats next to mine.

We became mates, hanging around together, laughing and smoking outside. He asked me if I had a passport, did I want to go away with him! I introduced him to Pauline because I liked him. He told her that he had genuine feelings for me which put her at ease.

Sadly though, he definitely groomed me, was out for all he could get. He tried over and over to get me to go to Amsterdam for him, not with him, it was always that he would meet me there. I was really not sure what to do so I rang Sheila. When she came round I told her everything and she told me very clearly that I was not going anywhere for him or with him. She said it was likely that he wanted me to do something illegal – what!! How did I not see that one coming……………ffs.

Very soon after, the lad disappeared without a word. A Police detective came to talk to staff. They had been watching his movements in Blackburn because he was heavily involved in drugs. He'd been in the hospital saying he had mental health problems and that's how he ended up in the flat next to mine. I suspect that he was faking the illness to avoid people he owed money to, but I'll never know for sure.

Staff told the Police that I had been friends with the lad so they came to ask me some questions. I told them he wanted me to get a passport and to go to Amsterdam. The lady detective told me that he was a very bad man, bad news, and that I needed to stay well away from him if he ever contacted me.

Not long after she came again, this time to tell me that the lad had been picked up by Police when he came back from Amsterdam carrying drugs. He had been sent to prison for a very long time but, I did recently hear that he was out again but thankfully living a long way from here. That's been the only major blip I've had since I left hospital. Nothing else comes close!

Not long after that, Sheila asked me if I would do a bit of work with her to slowly work towards me being discharged from mental health services. The level of panic that I felt was off the fucking scale!! She tried to tell me that it was because I was doing so well that I didn't need to be under mental health services anymore! My only thought was that I wouldn't see Sheila anymore. I felt like we were friends and I didn't want to have to face that.

Sheila assured me that we would stay in touch post discharge but I knew it wouldn't be the same. I agreed to do the work she wanted me to do. We actually worked on my anxiety that always came back whenever I was faced with a change that I didn't like. We worked on some tactics that I could use and I did actually feel that they might be useful.

I agreed that Sheila could use some of the work we did on my anxiety as part of a case study for her Master of Science degree in Applied Mental Health. I was so chuffed with my part in that and it felt a bit like I was giving her something back for all the help she had given me.

After over two years in my flat, I went with Sheila to my final out-patient review with the community psychiatrist, the same one who had said I was bound to relapse. Proved him wrong there didn't I!!! They decided between them that because I had been stable for so long, my medication could be reviewed by my GP in future and I could be discharged from mental health services!

I knew that was the plan but still, the range of emotions for someone who was born with no feelings was bloody unbelievable.

As part of the review, Sheila had rung Jake for his opinion. He said that the change in his mum in the last few years had been bloody brilliant, and he felt that he had his mum back! How bloody brilliant was that!

Jake's wedding

It is now over ten years ago when I was discharged from mental services – that still sounds unreal! Sheila called in from time to time for a brew. She helped me with any forms I needed filling in and she even went with me to any benefits reviews that I had to go to. Anything like that still terrified me but if I had somebody with me who knew what they were talking about, it made all the difference.

Jake recently got me tickets to see the boy band Westlife. We always had their songs on whenever he picked me up to go to his house, singing at the top of our voices! I'd never been to a real concert so couldn't believe I had tickets. When it got to the day, Jake remembers me struggling to get on the train! I danced from one foot to the other and he asked me what I was doing! I just couldn't get on until he more or less picked me up and put me onboard. Once I was on, everything was fine and that ended up being one of the best nights of my life despite the initial anxiety. Had I been on my own I probably would never have got on that train and have missed out on a brilliant experience. Sadly, that's what anxiety can do, rob you of happy times.

In 2014 Sheila left the mental health team to move to a new job with the NHS, but still in mental health. That was when she felt able to relax into our friendship.

Sheila writes a bit again. Despite the disparity in our relationship when I was her social worker, Susan and I had developed a comfortable friendship. Once she was no longer under mental health services, and I moved to my new job, I would pop in for a brew and we would have a catch up, without me feeling as if I might have been blurring any boundaries.

I had invested a lot into Susan's recovery and it would probably have been difficult to cut ties completely. Obviously I invested a lot into the other people on my case load but I had allowed myself to become Susan's friend. That could not have continued had I not changed my job at that time or had she not been well enough to be discharged. Susan would occasionally ring me with a problem such as getting her benefits sorted and I would go over on a day off to help get it resolved.

As a psychiatric social worker my therapeutic approach was always person centred. Research has consistently shown that the workers who exhibit warmth, empathic understanding and genuine interest, lay the foundation for effective therapeutic outcomes. I always felt lucky that my personality and personal values were reflected in social work values so it made my job much easier. I had a genuine interest in people and their story and hopefully that came across to the people who were on my caseload over the years.

One of the things I was always going on at Susan about for many years, was her teeth, or the little stumps that she had left! She was so much smarter now than she had ever been on the ward. She took care of her appearance and enjoyed buying new clothes. She had her hair done and wore make up so her lack of teeth just spoilt the overall look, but she was still terrified of going to see a dentist and there was nothing I could say or do to change her mind!

In November 2014, just before Jake and Leanne were due to get married, Susan rang me out of the blue and said she needed me to go round to her flat. I was expecting to have to fill a form in for something. When she opened the door, she was grinning like a Cheshire cat, with a full set of teeth!

She had finally plucked up the courage to go to a local dentist all by herself! She had had all of the rotten stumps of teeth removed and been fitted with a full set of dentures. Her face was transformed! She looked amazing! She was completely unrecognisable as that same woman who looked like she had escaped from an asylum, the day I first met her and I was bursting with pride for the woman she had become. Her lost years were behind her.

Many years on, Susan and I remain firm friends. We laugh a lot, a precious thing for someone who told me she was a living corpse born with no feelings!

Not long before I retired Susan began to say that she was thinking about writing a book but had no idea how to go about it. We researched ghost writers on the internet but found that would be very expensive! Gradually we came to the idea that I would have a bash at writing her story.

We applied for Susan's NHS notes, boxes and boxes of them and spent months going through them to find things relevant to her story. She talked about her childhood and the thread of death that ran through her life and her delusions. We met regularly, her talking, me writing. We were often joined by Pauline and the two of them would natter away about the years they've been friends, howling at some of their memories!

Sheila, Sue and Pauline

I never put any pressure on Susan to do this, it was her idea, but I'm so glad I've been involved! At the end of each session when she had been talking through her history, we would always have time for her to come back to the present day, making sure there were no lingering sadness or upset that might have a negative impact on her mood.

Jake speaks lovingly about his mum, and she is clearly an integral part of his family. He sees no point in dwelling on the past, just on the here and now. The only person responsible for your life is the person looking back at you from the mirror he says. He is a credit to both his mums, Susan and Pauline.

Of course, Susan must have the final words of her story to date.

I have purpose in my life which is so important. I am happy with the person I am. I don't dwell on the past because what is the point, it's gone, past. My family mean everything to me. In terms of family and being loved, I'm the richest woman alive.

My story goes on day to day. I'm not completely independent because I really don't think I would live anywhere else other than my supported living flat. I still have to take medication because the thought of relapse is just too bloody scary, but I'm quite happy to do it. Recovery is about reaching a point where life is as good as it is ever going to be when living with a mental illness.

My physical health is not as good as it could have been, but it doesn't really restrict me in many things. I can't walk very far without being out of breath but I've got inhalers, good medical support and I just have to be careful that's all.

Overall, looking back to the 1980's, I'm a very different woman, with lots of feelings! I'm not immortal but don't want to test that out, and I'm definitely not a living corpse!

Thank you for reading my story. I really hope that it can help someone, even a little bit. It is possible to recover and to live with mental illness, especially if you have the right medication and the right support.

Keep going, wherever you are in your personal recovery journey and I wish you everything good in life.

Sue Kelly

I will be eternally grateful to the numerous NHS and Social Services staff who tried to help me. To the staff at Balfour, especially Katrina and to Lucy Puzon for my cover photo make up. Huge thanks to David and Gwen at Publish

Nation. Finally, to Jake and his family, to Pauline and Sheila for their part in my story, I love you all.

A letter from Emily age 17

I saved her, and she saved me.
I'll always be a Nana's girl…
I don't feel well? I need her.
I feel sad? I need her cuddles.
Need to talk? I will ring her.
Need advice? Okay I'm going to ask her.
I'm struggling? Don't worry, she will help.

All I remember being told when I was little from Mum and Dad was 'you saved Nana' but I never really thought about it. I was a child, I had no idea about life and the perspective of things like I do now.

She knew that I was born before anybody told her.

She turned up to the hospital ward with flowers and a balloon for my Mum Leanne. My mum asked her 'do you want to hold Emily' and from being told when I was younger, and all I know is that my Nana looked at me and stroked me, then said 'I don't want to hurt her little soul'. Since my birth, Nana has turned into the most kind hearted woman in my life, To think of how far my Nana has come in life really does make you realise, things get better and SHE has proved that everything works out in the end and there IS a way out of the darkness..

There really isn't a bond like mine and hers, it's a different type of love. She's my safe place, my soulmate.. a soulmate doesn't have to be a partner or a friend, it's someone who inspires you to be a better person, the one person in the world that knows you better than anyone else, someone you carry with you forever. And without her in my life, I wouldn't be the Emily I am today

To think of how lucky I am to have a Nana like mine. Any time I'm in doubt she will always talk about how lucky and appreciative she is to have me in her life, I saved her in no way a person has ever been saved before.

I'm incredibly proud of her and I couldn't appreciate her any more than I already do.

If I've learnt anything from my Nana it would be to stay strong even if it's a bad day, a bad day doesn't mean a bad life.

A letter from Leasey, age 12

I love my Nan. She's always been the best she can be whenever me or my siblings are around. She never likes to see me without money so anytime my friends go out she makes sure to give me the same everybody else has got so I'm not the odd one out . She's amazing .

When I was younger, I remember each Wednesday she would always wait for me at the school gates with my mum, with a surprise for me . I always looked forward to coming out of school on a Wednesday to see my Nana. Any time I was down she made me feel 10x better with playing dolls with me . We would sit for hours on end playing with my Barbie's that she had bought me . Looking back now, she really gave me everything I wanted and still does.

On my birthdays, Nan always spoils me. Same goes for my brothers and sister. At Christmas time , she always spends a fortune on me and everybody else which I'm so thankful for. I honestly don't know what I'd do without her. A few Christmases ago, she bought just me and her tickets for Beauty and the Beast at Manchester Palace Theatre. That was the best thing she could do. So, on that day we took a train and had a day together. I love making memories with my Nan .

Now I'm older, things have changed . I don't see her as much as I used to as I'm always out with my mates.

My twin brothers absolutely adore my Nan. They look forward to seeing her after school. When it's a day she doesn't come they scream and cry because they want Nana Susan. It takes quite a while to calm them down.

As my Nan's got older, she's always been there for our family. I tell her everything- she tells me everything. Anytime we go out together or I sleep at hers, we always sit for hours just talking about how school is and how her days are. She always asks how my friends are doing. She honestly is the most caring lady I know and I love her so much for that.

Every other day, she loves to go into town with her friends and sits for at least an hour drinking her coffee and having something to eat .

I adore my Nana Susan . She adores me. I'm always excited to see her. She's my best friend and our bond could never be broken. I'm so proud of how far she has come with where she started and where she is now doing the best of her ability . I'm so lucky to have her in my life and without her I don't know what we would do.

More childhood – additional stories of a Blackburn childhood

When writing, I opened up a lot of everyday memories from my childhood. Not all of them are relevant to my mental illness but I think they are interesting from a social history perspective so we decided to include them at the end as additional reading.

I was a very skinny child but one of my best friends was a bit plumper and I wanted to be like her because I felt so skinny! One Christmas we both got doll's prams and a baby doll each and we played out every day, walking our prams round the block, pretending to feed our dolls and change them, put them back in the pram. Another Christmas we both got bikes. Obviously at the time, I had no idea how difficult it must have been for my parents to afford such luxuries.

Me and my skinny Catholic friend, not the plump one, would have little sales at the corner of our street, laying out a blanket and selling our old toys etc. We made quite a bit of money and went to the sweet shop a few streets away and spent our sixpences there.

We played skipping, hoola-hoops and hopscotch as well as with our dolls, just like all the other kids who played out all the time.

At weekends my mum would take us all to Beechwood Gardens in Blackburn. It was a long walk there and back.

We had butties, that my mum had made, and we were allowed to go on a few rides on the little fairground before walking back. The swing boats were my favourite, gradually working up the momentum until we felt like we were flying!

I do have lots of good memories of my childhood. As you can tell from my random memories, things were very different then! I remember the smell of warm pies when you walked past the bakery. My mum would occasionally get us a cake each, which was amazing. The grocer's next door to the baker's, sold everything you could imagine. It was old and dusty inside and the grocer wore a white pinny as he stood behind the big, long counter.

There was also a butcher's shop on that row. Everything you needed from two or three shops in a row, just round the corner from us, and typical of most towns at that time. All purchases would be put in a brown paper bag or wrapped in newspaper or put straight into my mum's shopping bag. No plastic carrier bags then!

As kids, we would often be sent to the local shops on errands to get things for my mum. We would buy food almost daily and it was used on that day, not kept like we do today. I remember my mum making a good broth, with dumplings in it. I don't think we ever owned a fridge or a washer. We would take our dirty washing to the local laundrette in my sister's old pram.

I remember the smell of bedding that had been dried outside and lines of terry towelling nappies blowing in the breeze, drying on the washing line whenever we were playing out in the back garden. I still love the smell of fresh bedding that has been dried outside and how it can take you back in time!

Very few people that I knew, owned their own house, we all had a rent book and the rent man would come to collect the money, with his brown leather satchel over his shoulder, every week.

My mum had several stepsisters who would regularly come round to ours. She was particularly close to two of them but I remember them being quite miserable and boring, drinking black tea and they all had yellow fingers and yellow around their mouths. I didn't understand what caused the yellow at the time but obviously I know now, having been a heavy smoker myself for many years before giving up! Her stepbrothers had moved to London as soon as they were old enough to leave Blackburn.

Bonfire night was a big thing in the 60's. When we made a Guy to go on the bonfire on November 5th, a lad came and popped the balloon we had made for its' head.

Pauline and I once cut each other's hair. My fringe ended up looking like Dave Hill's from the pop group Slade. We don't remember who did whose first but it was a laugh. Pauline says I was a lovely person when we were in our teens. If pushed I dare say she would say I still am!

I loved Donny Osmond but Pauline was a fan of David Cassidy. Everyone loved the Bay City Rollers though!

We had a lot of good times at school. On a weekend we would go into town as a group of four or five of us and look round the shops. We would go into Chelsea Girl, one of our favourites, and into Tommy Ball's where we would buy new shoes and chuck our old ones off the bridge!

We would mess about having photos taken, in the booths near the market. What a shame I don't have any of those now! I know for a fact that my granddaughters look like I did when I was their age.

We would always finish off in town with a potato pie, peas and gravy. I've no idea where I got my money from, unless it was pocket money.

Pauline modelled the jeans we made at the factory. They were going to take her to London for a business promotion because she was stick thin so an ideal model, but then she got pregnant, and fat. That was the end of her modelling days!

When she had her baby, I would go and help out with him, taking him out in his pram, or sometimes to the pub. I wasn't the best child minder because I was too soft with him!

When I left school I really struggled to hold a job down and regularly moved to somewhere new, as you could in the in those days! After the jeans factory I had moved to the job in a handbag factory. Jobs were easy to come by for unskilled workers in those days.

Fuck knows where I had learned to sew to a standard where I got a job, after the failed products of my school sewing lessons ended up in the bin. A shoe factory I worked in with a mate, was so cold that we wore our gloves and scarves while machining. It was a massive factory with loads of industrial sewing machines, same as the jeans factory. There were big holes in the wall which nobody ever explained, though the building was probably almost derelict.

The boss there was a tart of a woman. She once came out of the toilets holding up a soiled sanitary pad, saying "which one of you fan like fannies left this in the bathroom". I think my mate and I knew from day one that we wouldn't be staying there.

We decided to go in late one day and thought we'd got away with it so did it again the next day. We saw the tart approaching our machines and she shouted at us to get in the office! She asked where we had been when we should've been here at work! I asked her if she was going to sack us and she said, "too bloody right I'm sacking you, get out of my fuckin' factory." I knocked over a massive bin on the way out and shouted good riddance to her!

When I was a young teen, some of my mates came to wake me up one evening when I'd got into bed early. She said that there was a carload of her mates going down to see Barry Sheen in Wales. I took blankets and coats to keep warm as it was bloody freezing outside and the car didn't have a heater. The bloke who was driving, took us all the way to Swansea where Barry Sheen was meant to be. WTF was that all about!! The madness of youth!

I felt scared sat in the back of the car and told the big nosed bastard who was driving that he was going too fast. He pulled over and told us two to get out, in the middle of nowhere. I blamed my friend for getting us into such a mess, all so she could see one of her idols.

We eventually found a Police Station, no thanks to Google Maps which hadn't been invented, but to old fashioned road signs and asking people for directions. The Policeman behind the desk looked at us as if we were aliens and asked where the bloody hell we had crawled out from. We gave him our addresses in Blackburn and told him the story of how we came to be stranded in Swansea in the middle of the night.

Local Police were sent to our respective houses and our parents informed of the situation. My Dad said I could fuckin' well stop there! Fortunately, Carol's dad was more sympathetic and somehow sent the money for us to get home. I never forgave that big nosed bastard who was driving, for leaving us in the middles of nowhere, even when he later married my best mate, Pauline!

Me and my mate Carol had been abroad to Lloret de Mar at some point in the late 70's and we had a brilliant time so I soon agreed, when it was suggested, that five of us save up and go to Benidorm. However, I felt that something wasn't quite right from the outset, but not able to put my finger on it, I tried to join in the fun. While we were out in town on the first night, the lot of them fell out with me. I still don't know to this day what I did to upset them! I think I was maybe just the weakest link, easy to pick on.

We had to carry on sharing the place we were staying in, which felt horrible. The next night I went out on my own and when I came back all of my clothes and stuff had been thrown over the balcony. I gathered as much up as I could and trundled back to the bar. I had met up with two lovely girls from Germany, who spoke excellent English, and they had invited me to join them. When I told them why I was on my own they said I could go and stay with them, which

I did! They introduced me to another of their friends, a gorgeous lad who worked in the German post office.

We all spent the rest of the holiday together and had a brilliant time. No sex, just a good time hanging out together in the sunshine. They said I could stay with them. I went back to the apartment where my so called mates were, to get the rest of my stuff, but ended up staying the night, no idea why unless my drink was spiked. They had loads of lads in there and it seemed like an orgy going on.

I later overheard that they had taken photos of me while I was asleep but I've no idea if that was true or what the photos were of, if they even existed. I was scared that they might be indecent but thankfully they never appeared. Maybe someone still has them somewhere!

While in Benidorm I had a very vivid dream, so clear that I can remember it still. I think it was the night I had gone back to the original apartment. It wasn't that long after my brother had died and while asleep, I saw him, far off in the distance. It took me ages to walk towards him and as I got closer, I realised that he was sitting in front of some huge, partly open, iron cemetery gates.

I saw all of the "mates" I'd come on holiday with, going through the gates and started to follow them but my brother stopped me. He said that I didn't need to go through and I had to go back. He said I shouldn't be like them. When I woke up, I went to say goodbye to my new German friends and thanked them for allowing me to be part of their holiday. They asked for my address as they were hoping to visit the UK later that year.

I got a flight back on my own. I don't think I saw any of those so called local mates ever again except the main one who came round to collect a skirt she had left at mine, but I didn't want to see her and stayed upstairs. She wrote to me when I lost my baby a few years later, but I didn't reply. You don't treat mates like that and expect to still be mates at the end of it.

A few months later I got a postcard telling me that the three German friends were in London but didn't have enough money for a train to Blackburn. When I told my Dad who I had spent my holiday with and who the card was from, he went ballistic. He said I had no idea what went on in the war, but then didn't tell me either! Had he been a bit more accepting, I might have gone to London to meet up with them again. Instead, I wrote to them and thanked them again for looking after me on the holiday, and sadly never had contact with them again.

Jake remembers photos that his Grandad had on the wall, of his four grandchildren. Three of them were wearing their caps and gowns from graduating with university degrees, and Jake in the middle with a can of lager! His grandad said that he was most proud of Jake because the others might have degrees but they could never have survived everything that Jake had been through!

I hope that you have enjoyed these additional memories, many of which seem funny now but were just ordinary life back in the day.

Sue xx

A note about the author

Sheila Jump is a retired mental health practitioner, who specialised for the last ten years of her career, in older adults' mental health as part of the Rapid Intervention and Treatment Team under Lancashire & South Cumbria NHS Foundation Trust. She has a BA(Hons) in English and Linguistics (UCLAN) and qualified as a psychiatric social worker from the University of Manchester in 1996, gaining a Diploma in Social Work and a Diploma in Psychiatric Social Work. She went on to gain a MA in Gerontology (Salford) and an MSc (merit) in Applied Mental Health (Manchester), was an AMHP and a Best Interest Assessor.

www.ingramcontent.com/pod-product-compliance
Lightning Source LLC
Chambersburg PA
CBHW051112050726
47592CB00002B/790